Paul: Saint of the Inner City

Joseph P. Fitzpatrick, S.J.

Paulist Press
New York ♦ Mahwah

Scriptural quotations are from THE JERUSALEM BIBLE, 1966 edition.

Library of Congress Cataloging-in-Publication Data

Fitzpatrick Joseph P.
Paul : saint of the inner city / by Joseph P. Fitzpatrick.
p. cm.
ISBN 0-8091-3129-3
1. Bible. N.T. Epistles of Paul—Criticism, interpretation, etc. 2. Bible. N.T. Acts—Criticism, interpretation, etc. 3. Paul, the Apostle, Saint—Contributions to apostolate to city churches. 4. City churches—Mediterranean Region. 5. City churches—Biblical teaching. I. Title.
BS2655.C57F58 1990
225.9′2—dc20 89-38419
CIP

Published by Paulist Press
997 Macarthur Boulevard
Mahwah, NJ 07430

Printed and bound in the United States of America

Contents

Introduction

"The Saint of the Inner City," I call him. That's where he could be found, where he brought the good news of Jesus to the poor, the humble, the slaves, the outcasts in the great cities of the Roman empire: Antioch, Ephesus, Philippi, Thessalonica, Colossae, Athens, Corinth, Rome. It sounds like a travel schedule for commercial caravans, of trading ships, of military legions moving to and from their assigned stations. Paul was there.

In our day, here in the United States, the "inner city" is a challenge to the church, not unlike the challenge of the inner cities of the Roman empire. In New York, Philadelphia, Boston, Chicago, Detroit, Miami, Saint Louis, San Antonio, El Paso, Los Angeles and many others, in the worn out, beaten up, often abandoned sections of the inner city, are found the poor of our day. No longer slaves, they are the modern poor, older residents who have been around for generations but are still on the margins of our society: blacks from the American south or the Caribbean, newcomers from the Latin world and from Asia either fleeing violence and oppression or seeking a better life, many of them so-called "illegal" immigrants, living a hidden existence in the shadows, large numbers of them Catholics. There they are in the inner city, and we search for some social program or pastoral method that would enable us to help them to become part of our world. Most of all we need a role model, a hero, someone to show the way or who has met a similar challenge at other times, in other places. And we have him in Saint Paul.

This little book is an effort to describe him as "The Saint of the Inner City." It is not a theological treatise or a biblical commentary; it is not a scholarly history.[1] It is a series of reflections on some obvious features of Paul's life as he traveled from city to city, met with Jew and Gentile, slave and free, Roman and barbarian, people of many nations, of many cultures, of many styles of life. And many of them were the poor of the inner city where Paul met them.

What were they like? How did Paul deal with them? What success did he have? What does he have to tell us or show us about our approach to the people of our inner cities? He himself tells us a great deal about it; Luke tells us about it also. And bits and pieces of history can be added to describe the setting more clearly. It adds up to his vision, his courage, his love for the people to whom he brought his message, his tireless effort, his determination, his suffering, his painful disappointments, his successes. Therefore, we think about our own inner cities, and reflect about the experience of Paul, and pray to him and to the Lord for the vision and courage we need to bring the good news to the inner cities of our day as he brought it to the inner cities of his.

Paul came from Tarsus, "no mean city" as he called it. His Hebrew name was Saul. He was a member of what we would call today a "minority group," a member of one of the small Jewish communities of the diaspora who had established themselves in cities around the empire as teachers, merchants, bankers and brokers, and what we would call today "consultants," knowledgeable and experienced people who could advise others about foreign trade, the management of money, the development of trade. Like others of his time, he took a Roman name, Paul, to use in Roman cities and Roman situations; he had his Hebrew name, Saul, for use among his own people. How familiar to us today, aware of the problem of the names of newcomers, is the tendency of many to change their name lest they be identified as a foreigner. And with the Jewish minorities of his day, there were the strains, the insecurities, the intergroup tensions so familiar to us. The reaction of the Jews, historically, has been twofold. Some went out of their way to separate themselves from their Hebrew customs, to adopt a Roman or Greek style of life, to "make it" in a Gentile world. Many who did this were repudiated by their own people; they were seen as betrayers, traitors to the traditions of the Hebrew people. The other reaction was an effort to cling tenaciously to their Hebrew ways, to segregate themselves from the Gentile world, apart from their business dealings with it. This was the situation in which Paul had grown up. He knew what it meant to live as a minority in a world that was culturally different. And he faced the tensions and insecurities that were common to his people.

His experience as a Jew in the Gentile world was to be a major factor in his apostolate. He knew Greek, he had lived in a Gentile city, he was familiar with Gentile ways. Thus, when Gentiles began to become Christians, the apostles called on him to do what they could not do—bring the good news of Jesus in a language and a style that would make sense to the Gentile world.

> The church in Jerusalem heard about this [the growth of the church in Antioch] and they sent Barnabas to Antioch. . . . Barnabas then left for Tarsus to look for Saul, and when he found him he brought him to Antioch (Acts 11:22–26).

Antioch, the administrative center of the Roman occupation of the near east, was a combination of Miami,

Washington, Hollywood and New York. It was famous for its athletes and its shows, a center for "first nights," critics, tourists, revelers; lights, colonnades, fountains—a Roman paradise. It had liquor and sex, ulcers, frayed nerves, insanity, suicide—a typical center of Roman occupation, enjoyment and trade. Romans lived on the hills overlooking the Mediterranean, haughty, domineering, masters of the world. Jews were there, jealous of their tradition. Greeks had their culture; they were the teachers, paid by the Romans to provide the culture that Rome did not have; they were teachers of the Romans, cynical and critical, but subservient. Syrians, Egyptians, Indians, Persians—all were there at this crossroads of commerce, politics, competition for wealth and power, intrigue. There were teamsters, tanners, longshoremen, seamen, candlemakers, tradesmen of all nations and walks of life, a busy, active, turbulent city. The apostles, all Jews, did not know what to do with Christians in this kind of confused setting. They sent Barnabas who came from the Greek world; he had been born in Cyprus. And Barnabas went to find Saul, and they both went to Antioch, apostles of the inner city. What was Paul to do? What did God want him to do with this strange world where people from all backgrounds had begun to hear of Jesus Christ?

Corinth was another kind of city, on a narrow isthmus that linked the great sea lanes of the west with those of the east. It was a strategic city for commerce as well as a strategic location for military communications. It had been a city of great beauty in its heyday, but it had been destroyed in conquest and rebuilt by Julius Caesar. It was nothing of its former self in the days of Paul. It was a Roman colony, with little of Greek character. It was a city of shipping and commerce. In this sense, like

Antioch, it had its teamsters, longshoremen, seamen, warehouses, with all the paraphernalia and activity of a busy port city. By the time of Paul it had deteriorated and it had a poor reputation for morals; the nickname for a prostitute was "Corinthian girl." It was rough, tough and commercial. It was also the center of the Isthmian games, and devotees of the games would flock to Corinth to see them. But Corinth had its inner city, its poor, its strangers, its unemployed seamen waiting for and hoping for a job on the next ship. It was hardly a place where one would expect to find a group of people who showed much promise for religious and spiritual development. Corinth was the one city where Paul seems to have been afraid, possibly ready to quit the city. But "one night the Lord spoke to Paul in a vision: 'Do not be afraid to speak out, nor allow yourself to be silenced. I am with you. I have so many people on my side in this city that no one will attempt to hurt you'" (Acts 18:9–11). A great following in Corinth! This is what the Lord was saying. In that poor city of such ill repute, a kind of backwash of the Roman empire, "a great following" was waiting for the word of God. And Paul stayed for eighteen months and, out of that unpromising inner city, he was to develop one of the great centers of the early church.

How did he do this? What gave him the vision that these poor people, struggling for existence in the great cities, often exploited and oppressed, had the potential to become the founders of the new communities of Christians? This, indeed, would be a sign for us, a sharing of the vision that Paul had, the capacity to see, in the hearts and minds of people whom the world called worthless, "what the world holds as 'nothings'" as Paul described them in his first letter to the Corinthians, the capacity to develop into dedicated followers of Jesus

Christ. This is the vision we need in our own inner cities as we search for a method of evangelization that would enable us to find in our own inner cities the persons of similar spiritual and religious potential, who could develop into the great communities of Christians in our day.

The reflections of the following chapters are an effort to capture some of the vision and spirit of Paul. We will follow him on his journeys, listen to what he tells us in his letters, reflect on his behavior in the inner city, pray for insight into his missionary style, and hope that God will give us a similar insight that we need to fulfill our missionary vocation in the inner cities of our day.

Notes

1. This is not a book for which a lengthy or detailed bibliography is appropriate. Furthermore, most of the books on Saint Paul are scholarly discussions of his theology. The kinds of books that were helpful in the preparation of this manuscript include the following:

Raymond E. Brown, *The Community of the Beloved Disciple: The Life, Loves and Hates of an Individual Church in New Testament Times*, New York: Paulist Press, 1979.

R. E. Brown and J. P. Meier, *Antioch and Rome*, New York: Paulist Press, 1983. Probably the best available book about the controversy among the early Jewish Christians about the freedom of Gentiles from the Mosaic law.

Sherman E. Johnson, *Paul the Apostle and His Cities*, Wilmington, Delaware: Michael Glazier, 1987. This book is not as detailed or as scholarly as that of Wayne Meeks. It is brief, very easy to read and for the busy reader, perhaps more useful than the Meeks book.

Wayne A. Meeks, *The First Urban Christians*, New Haven: Yale University Press, 1983. This is really an ideal source book for a study of Paul's inner city ministry. It is one of the most detailed presentations of the sociological aspects of the people to whom he ministered.

Otto F. A. Meinardus, *Saint Paul in Greece*, Athens: Lycabettus Press, 1973. This is more a travelogue than a scholarly presentation. It is short and easy to read.

H. V. Morton, *In the Footsteps of Saint Paul*. This is an old but well respected book by a person well informed and with wonderful insights about the cities in which Paul ministered.

Jerome Murphy-O'Connor, O.P., *Saint Paul's Corinth, Texts and Archeology*, Wilmington, Delaware: Michael Glazier, 1983. This is an excellent presentation of all available ancient texts which describe life in Corinth. Very scholarly and very interesting.

1. Rise Up and Go into the City

"Rise up now and go into the city and you will be told what you have to do." And the Lord told Ananias to go to Paul ". . . because this man is my chosen instrument to bring my name before pagans and pagan kings and before the people of Israel" (Acts 9:15–16). It seemed to be all settled. Ananias visited Paul; Paul regained his sight, took some nourishment and began to preach. But years were to pass before it became clear to Paul what his mission was to be.

How could he know what to do? It did not break upon him like the flash of light that threw him from his horse. Many years were to pass before the meaning of the Lord's words were to become clear, that he would obey the command of the Lord to "bring my name before pagans and kings and before the people of Israel." He spent three years "in Arabia" after he fled from Damascus, and a long period in Tarsus where he had been sent by the apostles after they found him too troublesome to remain in Jerusalem. When and how was the Lord going to call him or make it clear how he was to bring the gospel to the pagans? How was he to learn the will of the Father?

These were days of prayer, of reflection, of waiting upon the Lord. Paul evidently knew that if he had trust and confidence, the Lord would eventually show him. But six or seven or ten years is a long time to wait. Yet he waited, the aggressive, fiery, determined Paul, waiting and praying for the Lord to show him what to do. Finally the call came. When Barnabas needed someone to help him with the Gentiles in Antioch, he remembered that Paul was in Tarsus. He went and called him and both went to Antioch. The great work of Paul was about to begin. Faith, confidence, prayer, waiting patiently, listening for the Lord's call—these were part of Paul's experience. He was finally shown the way.

Is this not the same problem all have as they face the challenge of a new or difficult ministry? Where shall I go, what shall I do, how shall I do it?

We face the inner city, a turbulent, rapidly changing center of new people, different ways of life, poverty and deprivation, bias and discrimination, drugs, thievery, unemployment, drunkenness, face-to-face with human courage, determination, generosity, endurance, trust in the Lord. What are we to do in this inner city? How are we to do it? If Paul's life is an example, it may be years before the Lord shows us the way. In the meantime, we have Paul's example: faith, prayer, patient waiting, listening for the Lord's call.

What is needed in the inner city is the vision that Paul had. In the presence of problems, conflict, controversy, hostility, he had the vision to see in the hearts and minds of the people the promise of deep faith, of generosity, of dedication to the service of the Lord and the Lord's followers. "I have a great following in that city," the Lord told Paul about Corinth when most people would have given it up as lost.

To see through the unpleasant appearances, the behavior we may judge as immoral, actions or attitudes that may strike us as uncivilized, to get beyond this to a perception of the goodness that may lie hidden beneath it all, this is the vision that we need in the inner city. We all have the tendency to judge others according to the norms that prevail in our way of life. I remember an incident in a Puerto Rican town which affected me long before I was aware of respect for other cultures. I had been encouraged to visit a parish where a new church had just been built; it was highly praised as an outstanding example of modern ecclesiastical architecture. It was certainly that. The proud pastor who had planned the church was showing me around. On the side was a small pedestal with a statue of our Lady. While we were there, a poor woman entered the church with a small bundle of flowers in her arms. She knelt fervently before the statue of our Lady, then placed the flowers at the base of the statue. Evidently this was her practice in the old church. As soon as she left, the pastor picked up the flowers and threw them unceremoniously out into the yard. I could appreciate the concern of the pastor for the appearance of his church. But something inside me was troubled. I thought of the widow's mite and wondered how the widow would have felt if the Levite had taken the mite and thrown it out into the street. The gift of the woman was evidently a gesture of great love, and had she known what had happened to her flowers I think she would have been hurt. Had the pastor recognized that? Were the flowers nothing more than a spoiling of the architectural environment, rather than a symbol of reverence and devotion to our Lady?

I mention this as a small item of failure to perceive the deeper meaning of a person's behavior: Was it messing up the church or a gesture of love of a poor woman? We must perceive, beneath the outward appearances, the deeper meaning of what a person does. "All that rings true; all that makes for right; all that is lovely in the telling, virtue and honor wherever virtue and honor may be found, let this be the argument of your thought," Paul taught the Philippians (Phil 4:8–9). It was the gift he had, to see beneath a misleading exterior to the truth or the beauty, or the virtue that lay beneath it. How did Paul achieve this? By prayer, reflection, patience, confidence in God, and deep faith in Jesus Christ. No matter what people looked like to the respectable of the world, said Paul, "you are neither Greek nor Hebrew, nor slave nor free, nor Roman nor Barbarian, but only Christ Jesus." His vision pierced through all outward appearances; he saw in others "only Christ Jesus," and this gave him the patience, the respect for others, the dedication to the preaching of the gospel that enabled him to be an effective apostle of the inner city.

So with ourselves. His example teaches us that if we are to be effective in the inner city, we must have the vision to see in others, neither white nor black, nor Asian nor American, nor learned nor unlearned, nor rich nor poor, but only Christ Jesus. And how is this achieved? Very much the way Paul must have achieved it, through his prayer, his reflection, his love for Jesus Christ, his dedication to the spirit of the gospel. If that is our method, we may be able to penetrate beyond the actions which may not be very impressive to that "which is true, that which is beautiful, that which is lovely in the telling; virtue and merit wherever virtue and merit may be found."

The Details of the Task: The Freedom of the Gentiles from the Mosaic Law

The importance of Paul's vision, and the prayer and patience whereby he developed it, becomes clearer when we look back at the details of the vocation to which God called him: "to bring my name before pagans and kings and before the people of Israel." Paul was a Jew in a Gentile world; that alone was a difficult task. We know much more now about the difficulties of minority groups, and Paul was one of the minority, bringing a new gospel and a new faith to the dominant population. More serious than that, his vocation was to minister to Gentiles during a major break from the religious traditions of the Jewish people. This repeatedly nearly got Paul killed.

The problem of ministry to Gentiles was to be a major problem for the first members of the Christian faith. The first followers of Jesus were all Jews. They came out of the religious tradition of the Hebrews, a profoundly sacred tradition based on the revelations of God to Abraham, Moses and the prophets. It was formalized by Moses in the law that he gave to the Hebrew people, and was sanctified in the covenant, affirmed in blood, that bound the people to the Lord as his chosen ones, entrusted with faith in the one true God and the promise of the savior whom God would eventually send. The Mosaic law which specified this religious tradition was really what anthropologists call a "culture," a complete way of life. The Mosaic law regulated every aspect of Hebrew life, what they could eat and how food was to be prepared, when they could work or take a journey, their relationship to Gentiles, the relationship of husband to wife (even to the detail of when they could have intercourse), the relation of parent to child, of master to servant. The temple, the sacrifices, the observances all constituted the framework of the covenant, the sacred bond between God and his people.

Jesus told his apostles: "Go, teach all nations," but no clear instructions were given as to how this was to be done. Therefore, when Cornelius, a Roman officer, appeared as the first Gentile to ask for baptism, the question arose: What were the apostles to do with Gentiles who wished to become Christian? Were they required to follow the Mosaic law, the only religious tradition the apostles knew? Were they to be circumcised, obliged to follow the observances of the Hebrew tradition? God settled the issue in the remarkable revelation to Peter (Acts 10) in which God clearly instructed Peter that Gentiles were not to be required to follow the Mosaic law. As Peter himself proclaimed in his address to Cornelius and his family: "The truth I have now come to realize is that God does not have any favorites, but that anybody of any nationality who fears God and does what is right is acceptable to him" (Acts 10:34-35). In other words, Gentiles were not to be required to become circumcised and to follow the Mosaic law. Romans were to remain Romans, Greeks were to remain Greeks. All were to give expression to the word and life of Jesus within the framework of their own culture and way of life, provided that they "feared God and did what is right." Peter instructed his companion disciples to baptize the family of Cornelius, and the Spirit of the Lord manifested itself in the behavior of the Gentiles equally as it had among the Jews.

This appeared to settle the issue decisively. Not so. This problem was to trouble the church throughout its history. It was the major issue at the first council of the church, the Council of Jerusalem (Acts 15), and it was to be a major issue in the Second Vatican Council as well. How was the life and faith of Jesus, the one true doctrine of salvation, to express itself in the manifold cultures of the Gentile world?

Peter received the revelation, but it was Paul who eventually carried it out. In doing so he faced the bitter hostility of the non-Christian Jews and serious controversy among the Christians as well. Paul even confronted Peter about the issue when Peter came to Antioch. When some of the Jewish Christians challenged Paul and the Gentiles and insisted that they must follow the Mosaic law, Paul referred the issue to Peter and the acknowledged leaders of the church. Paul's ministry was confirmed in the Council of Jerusalem (Acts 15).

> When Cephas came to Antioch, however, I opposed him to his face, since he was manifestly in the wrong. His custom had been to eat with the pagans, but after certain friends of James arrived, he stopped doing this and kept away from them altogether for fear of the group that insisted on circumcision. . . . When I saw they were not respecting the true meaning of the good news, I said to Cephas in front of everyone, "In spite of being a Jew, you live like the pagans and not like the Jews, so you have no right to make the pagans copy Jewish ways" (Gal 2:11–14).

This was only the beginning of the controversy, and Paul was in the midst of it. How did he know he was right? Why was he so convinced that his ministry was the one confirmed by God in the revelation to Peter?

Paul quickly realized that his vocation to the Gentiles would involve him in troublesome controversies that he had not anticipated. The issue was a most serious one, and it is easy to understand the reaction of many of the devout Jewish Christians. The Mosaic law was the only religious tradition the Jews had known. It was sealed in the covenant struck by Moses; if his people were faithful to the convenant, God promised to be favorable to them. The ancestors of the Jews had sacrificed, suffered and died in order to be faithful to the law and the covenant. It was the sacred and holy way of life revealed by God to Moses. And now Peter was telling Jewish Christians that it didn't bind them anymore. Gentiles could serve the Lord equally well and be bound to God through the new covenant in the blood of Christ. This was very difficult for many Jewish Christians to accept. They accepted the new covenant but saw no reason to reject the old.

Paul had the special vocation to minister to the Gentiles and protect their freedom as Christians; the requirements of the Mosaic law were not to be imposed on them. This was the very difficult task to which Paul had been called. Where did he get the vision, the insight, the spiritual stamina to be faithful to this vocation, even despite the controversy it provoked among many of the devout Jewish Christians of that time?

It is doubtful that any changes in our present day can compare with the change involved in the break with the Mosaic law. How then do we respond to the challenge of change in our day? Certainly as we face the apostolate of the inner city, there will be need for many changes in method, in the character of priestly or lay ministry, in style of life. As in the time of Paul, these religious changes touch the economic and political interests of many people and result in conflicts with political interests that rely for support in their claim to be the law of God. The termination of the sacrifice of lambs under the Mosaic law resulted in major financial losses to sheep farmers as well as to the priests who performed the sacrifice. A simple change in our day putting an end to the rule of abstaining from meat on Fridays for Catholics certainly had an impact on the people in the fish business.

How does a follower of Jesus know what conduct is required by the law of God? What behavior is the mark of the person who "seeks God and does what is right"? Paul had to resist the opposition of all, both Jews and Jewish Christians, who were convinced that the observance of the law and fidelity to the covenant were necessary for one seeking to serve the Lord in truth. Where did he get the vision and the strength to do it? It was evidently by prayer, by reflection, by penance and sacrifice. In the case of the Mosaic law he had the support of the authority of the apostles at the Council of Jerusalem assuring him that his ministry to the Gentiles was in conformity to the revelation given to Peter. But he faced the challenge of guiding the Gentiles in the way of the Lord as it was to be expressed in their own Roman, or Greek, or Egyptian or Syrian way of life. This was not to be easy.

At every moment he faced the wrath of the non-Christian Jews who threatened his life and attacked him with mobs from whom he had to escape or sometimes be rescued by the Roman soldiers. He also had to face the criticism of the Jewish Christians who devoutly clung to the religious tradition of the Mosaic law. But by the grace of God through prayer and sacrifice, he prevailed. "I am the least of the apostles. . . . I hardly deserve the name apostle, but that is what I am, and the grace that he gave me has not been fruitless. On the contrary, I, or rather the grace of God that is with me, has worked harder than any of the others" (1 Cor 15:9–10).

In the Gentile World, What Is Right?

So much for the Mosaic law. That was only one of Paul's problems. Paul was aware that the Gentile world was no model of virtue. Facing the problems of idolatry, sex, drunkenness, sensuality and a host of other vices, he had to decide what conduct was required by a follower of Jesus—what had to be condemned and avoided, what was to be accepted and encouraged. He was fierce in his condemnation of Roman society as he found it:

> God has abandoned them to degrading passions. . . . And so they are steeped in all sorts of depravity, rottenness, greed and malice, and addicted to envy, murder, wrangling, treachery and spite: libelers, slanderers, enemies of God, rude, arrogant and boastful, enterprising in sin, rebellious to parents, without brains, honor, love or pity (Rom 1:26–30).

He had to deal with the followers of Diana in Ephesus, the Christians who would not work in Thessalonica, the Corinthians who got drunk in the celebration of the eucharist, the Christians who faced all kinds of problems in a Roman world where food in the public markets had already been offered to the pagan gods. Yet he was strong in his exhortation: "Fill your minds with everything that is true, everything that is noble, everything that is good and pure, everything that we love and honor, and everything that can be thought virtuous and worthy of praise" (Phil 4:8).

Two things are clear in Paul's experience in the Gentile cities: He was no "uncertain trumpet"; he was severe in his condemnation of what he saw as evil, and he was intolerant of those who persisted in their rejection of the teaching of Jesus. At the same time, he never allowed the sinfulness of his people to blind him to their capacity for good, for the faith, for a Christian life. In his second letter to the Corinthians, he has this sad lament:

> What I am afraid of is that when I come I may find you different from what I want you to be, and you may find that I am not as you would like me to be; and then there will be wrangling, jealousy, and tempers roused, intrigues and backbiting and gossip, obstinacies and disorder. I am afraid that on my next visit, my God may make me ashamed on your account, and I shall be grieving over all those who have sinned before and have still not repented of the impurities, fornication and debauchery they committed (2 Cor 13:20–21).

Yet Paul did not abandon them as he abandoned the Athenians. "Do not be afraid to speak out," Jesus said to Paul. "I . . . have so many people on my side in that city that no one will attempt to hurt you" (Acts 18:9-10). He sought out that which was good and had the potential of virtue. He stayed with the Corinthians and eventually they became one of the great centers of the early church.

It is doubtful that, in our inner cities, we would find a situation as depraved as the Rome that Paul describes. But the problem of Paul in the Gentile cities remains, to some extent, in our own inner cities: drugs and sex, violence and exploitation, drunkenness and child abuse, irresponsibility. For one who wishes to focus on the evident evils, there is much in the inner city that leaves a modern apostle discouraged and frustrated. Nevertheless, if, like Paul in Corinth, we stay with it, never allowing the evils to obscure the good that lies latent there, eventually the working of the grace of the Lord will shine forth. The Lord can very well say to us in our inner cities: "I have so many people on my side in that city that no one will hurt you." If we are persistent enough, and trusting in the Lord, he will give us the grace to push aside the weeds and gather the harvest.

In this way, Paul serves as a model for those who minister to the people in the inner city. After three years of prayer in Arabia, and seven or more years waiting in Tarsus, praying and waiting on the Lord, when the call came, Paul had been prepared. Not everyone preparing for inner city ministry can take ten years of prayerful isolation and preparation. But if prayer permeates our lives, as it did his, we may have the vision we need to perceive the latent good in the people of the inner city, and the persistence to stay with the apostolate until, by God's grace, discouragement is transformed into fulfillment.

2. Antioch

Antioch was the third greatest city of the Roman empire at the time of Jesus and Paul. It was the administrative capital of the Roman occupation forces in the near and far east. It is clear then that we are talking of a city, great in size as well as importance. It had been founded in 300 B.C. by one of the generals of Alexander the Great; it was conquered and occupied by the Romans in 65 B.C.

It was a busy and strategic crossroads of the conflicting empires of the time, where military routes from Greece and Rome met the military forces of the middle east, of Syria, Persia and India. It was a center of commercial routes by land and sea from Africa to the north, and from the north to Syria, Palestine, and Africa. It was the commercial, political and military metropolis of the near east, outsized and outshone only by Alexandria and Rome.

Antioch was considered to be one of the most beautiful cities of the world in the time of Paul. The two main streets, north/south and east/west, were wide avenues, lined with colonnades that were illuminated at night; marginal roads flanked the main avenue on each side. The brilliant illumination at night was one of the wonders of the city. The Roman writer Libanius describes it:

> In Antioch at night, other lights replace the light of the sun. Day and night are distinguished only by the manner of the illumination. Busy hands scarcely notice the difference when night comes and men go on working undisturbed in

> the darkness. And, if anyone desires, he may go dancing and singing through the night, so that Hephaestus and Aphrodite share the night. (Quoted in J. Holzner, *Paul of Tarsus*, 1944, 81.)

An elegant suburb called Daphne was the center of recreation and revelries. The mansions of the officers of the Roman army of occupation and of wealthy leaders of politics and commerce spread out across the countryside. Near the mouth of the Orontes River was the seaport, Seleucia Pieria, where ships from all over the Mediterranean exchanged their cargo. It was a center of culture, boasting a famous library; it was a center of athletic games, dramatic presentations, and ritual celebrations to the numerous gods and goddesses of the Pantheon of the people of Antioch.

It was a center as well of political conflicts, intrigues, and corruption. Roman military officers and political officials, competitive businessmen, merchants, artists, athletes, leaders of religious cults—all intermingled in a city where the struggles for power, wealth, influence and prestige swirled around the city day and night. Also in great numbers were the poor, the slaves, men and women who did the menial work and who bore the burden of the manifold tasks that enabled a city like Antioch to function.

It was also a mixture of races and nationalities, of people from all parts of the world. A small colony of Jews lived in Antioch, respected for their religious lives and their commercial ability. As Christian Jews fled as refugees to Antioch and joined this Jewish community, the word and life of Jesus began to be spread and a flourishing Christian community began to grow in Antioch. One of the first deacons, Nicolaus, ordained to serve the

Christian community in Jerusalem, was a convert to Judaism from Antioch (Acts 6:5). Since the apostles knew no Greek, the common language in Antioch, and having had no experience dealing with the Gentile world, they sent Barnabas to minister to the church in Antioch. Barnabas had been born in Cyprus, had been brought up in the Gentile world, and spoke Greek. Barnabas then went to Tarsus to find Saul and brought Saul (Paul) with him to Antioch. Paul's renewed apostolic life took place there. After years of waiting and prayer, Paul's vocation as the apostle of the Gentiles was to become clear to him at Antioch.

The Acts of the Apostles tells us little about Paul's early days in Antioch. He certainly knew of the city; no one at all educated in those days could have been ignorant of it, any more than an American could be unaware of Chicago or a Frenchman about Paris. Barnabas brought Paul there for two obvious reasons. The Christian community was developing rapidly there and the apostles were evidently trying to provide the community with more preachers. When the persecution of the Christians broke out in Jerusalem after the execution of Stephen, some of the Christians left Jerusalem and came to Antioch. They joined the well-established Jewish community that lived there and began to preach about Jesus; "A large number of people were won over to the Lord" (Acts 11:23). "Some of them, however, who came from Cyprus and Cyrene [Gentile areas] started preaching to the Greeks." Thus there was also a growing community of Gentile Christians developing in Antioch as well. Paul's familiarity with the Gentile world and his ability to speak Greek would enable him to be a great help to the community in Antioch. The remarkable variety of the community is reflected in this early history.

Here were Christians from Cyrene, at a central point in North Africa, and from Cyprus, an island in the Mediterranean, preaching the gospel to the Gentiles of Antioch. A list of the prophets and teachers, as given in Acts (13:1) also reflects the variety. There was Barnabas from Cyprus, Simeon the black man, Lucius from Cyrene, Manaen who had been brought up in Palestine with Herod the tetrarch, and Saul the Jew from Tarsus. Here they were, in the midst of a metropolitan community, from all parts of the world, in the bustling, exciting, turbulent center of the eastern part of the Roman empire.

Antioch was a city of great wealth as well as poverty. Early in Paul's experience, we find him involved in a mission of charity to the Christians in Jerusalem. Famine struck the Roman empire in the years 46–48 A.D., according to the historian Josephus. The Christians in Antioch sent what relief they could to the Christians in Jerusalem. Paul and Barnabas were assigned to deliver the money to the elders of the church there. It is an interesting insight into the practical problems of poverty, so common in Paul's day, as it is in the inner cities of our own day. Repeatedly we find him collecting money for the relief of Christian brothers or sisters in a variety of cities, particularly Jerusalem where Christians seem to have had repeated problems of poverty.

Paul's first task was to protect the freedom of the Gentiles from the imposition of the Mosaic law. As indicated above, this was a focus of serious controversy in the early church. When some of the Jewish Christians continued to press the issue, Paul and Barnabas journeyed to Jerusalem to submit the question to the apostles. In that important meeting, reported in Acts 15, the apostles confirmed Paul's conviction and, in what is identified as the first council of the church, communicated their decision in writing to the Christians at Antioch. Two leading men of the Jerusalem church, Judas and Silas, delivered the letter. They were not to be troubled, nor were the Gentiles to be circumcised. They need not follow the Mosaic law nor the Hebrew ways. They were simply to abstain from fornication, from anything sacrificed to idols, from meat of strangled animals, and from blood.

This was simply one part of the major effort of Paul in Antioch, to proclaim the unity of all men and women in Jesus Christ, to break down the barriers between class, or race, or nationality. As he proclaimed to the Galatians: ". . . there are no more distinctions between Jew and Greek, slave or free, male or female, but all of you are one in Christ Jesus" (Gal 3:28). He repeats this theme in various ways throughout his entire ministry. Paul was not proclaiming a social policy, or a strategy to put an end to slavery as it existed in his day, or to change the structure of societies in which he lived and preached. He was really saying that their unity in Jesus transcended all their differences. The fact that they were slave or free, man or woman, Roman or barbarian, was not that important; what was important, and radically so, was the fact that they were one in Christ Jesus. Paul was not trying to transform all these people into one culture or way of life. He had resisted Peter for imposing Jewish ways on Gentiles. He had no intention of imposing a Roman way of life on Syrians or a Greek way of life on Africans. The point he was making was that their ethnic or racial or nationality differences were not to be a reason for separation or division or hostility. Transcending their separate national or ethnic or racial identities was the identity they all possessed in common, their identity as members of the body of Christ. It was this that enabled people of distinct races and nationalities to remain themselves, but to relate to each other as brothers and sisters in the Lord. Paul may not have known what a modern sociologist means by cultural pluralism, but his concept of the Christian community, many different people sharing the same life of Christ, was an actual example of it in Antioch.

This does not mean either that Paul was indifferent to exploitation or injustice. He insisted that they behave to one another as brothers and sisters in the Lord; there could be no injustice or exploitation possible if they did so. His beautiful exhortation in Colossians 3:12–17 reflects this: "You are God's chosen race, his saints; he loves you and you should be clothed in sincere compassion, in kindness and humility, gentleness and patience. Bear with one another; forgive each other as soon as a quarrel begins. . . . The Lord has forgiven you; now you must do the same. . . ." "Slaves, be obedient to the men who are called your masters in this world. . . . Masters, make sure that your slaves are given what is just and fair, knowing that you too have a master in heaven" (Col 3:22–4:1). If men and women lived this way, Paul was convinced there would be no injustice.

In a sense, Paul was not sensitive as we are today to what we call "unjust social structures," social institutions which function in such a way that the benefits of society are not evenly or fairly or justly distributed. Paul never wrote anything comparable to the pastoral letter on war and peace (1983) or the pastoral letter on the American economy (1987), but the principles of Christian living that he preached permeate these modern statements. In other words, if men and women are not inspired to live as Paul exhorted them, as brothers and sisters in the Lord, there is little likelihood of effective social reform as it is understood today. It is precisely the reading of the scriptures that has inspired the demands for social justice in Central and South America. The militant response to the question "Am I my brother's keeper?" has resulted in an emphatic demand for social change. The pastoral letter on interracial relations, "Brothers and Sisters to Us" (1986), touches upon personal attitudes more directly, but we know what blacks mean when they speak of "institutional racism," namely institutions which function in such a way that whites are favored and blacks are not.

Of course, we live in a society in which democratic processes have prevailed, and the possibility of changing social structures by legislation is well understood. In Paul's day, Roman emperors ruled the world in which Paul lived. There was not much chance of changing things unless someone could marshal a military power to challenge the Roman legions. Paul was well aware of this. His journeys through the empire were possible because the Roman army had built the roads. He could sail the Mediterranean without fear of pirates because the Roman galleons had driven the pirates out. Rome guaranteed its citizens basic rights, and Paul repeatedly took advantage of them. "I am a Roman citizen," he insisted on numerous occasions, and he was spared the punishments that were visited on the subjects in occupied territories. One thing he did not have was a representative in the Roman senate for whom he had voted and through whom he could exercise advocacy for social change as we can. In our day, access to the vote and to political influence places a responsibility on us that did not exist in Paul's time. Thus the exhortation of the bishops to fulfill our responsibilities by participating in the political process is a religious perspective which Paul would not have been aware of.

Paul was overwhelmed by the new spirit of Jesus.

He had grown up in the Hebrew tradition in which the covenant had been made between God and the Hebrew people. The Gentiles had no place in it. The fact that the new covenant in the blood of Jesus was to embrace the entire world left Paul amazed at the infinite goodness of God and its meaning for the Gentile world. "Do not forget, then, that there was a time when you who were pagans . . . had no Christ, and were excluded from membership in Israel, aliens with no part in the covenants with their promise; you were immersed in the world, without hope and without God" (Eph 2:11–13). And he continues his statement in joy: "For he is the peace between us, and has made the two into one and broken down the barrier which used to keep them apart, actually destroying the hostility caused by the rules and decrees of the law" (Eph 2:14). And he finishes: "So you are no longer aliens or foreign visitors; you are citizens like all the saints, and part of God's household."

Paul was filled with wonder. "I throw myself on my knees," he said in his awareness of this mystery which " . . . now revealed through the Spirit to his holy apostles and prophets was unknown to any men in past generations; it means that pagans now share the same inheritance, that they are parts of the same body, and that the same promise has been made to them in Christ Jesus through the gospel" (Eph 3:5–7). One can imagine Paul, in Antioch, with that mixed population around him, Romans, and Greeks, and Syrians, and Egyptians, slaves, draymen, seafarers, merchants, artists, athletes, scholars, and he calls out to them:

> . . . no room for distinction anymore between Greek or Jew, between the circumcised or uncircumcised, between the barbarian or the

> Sythian, between slave and free. There is only Christ and he is everything and he is in everything (Col 3:11).

This was the first Gentile church. With all its turmoil and controversy, the gospel was being preached, and a varied population of rulers and ruled, of oppressors and oppressed, of wealthy and poor, became aware of the gift of God's life given to them through Jesus, and the new covenant in the blood of Christ that made them one. The South Bronx and South Chicago and Central Newark and Detroit are not Antioch. They are the poor sections, the inner city of the great and wealthy metropolitan centers of our day. Many of them have heard the gospel message. People gather in the black churches, the Hispanic parishes, the Pentecostal storefronts. They wonder why the message they hear in the gospel is not given expression in the neighborhoods where they live. Many others, living without hope, take to drugs or crime and might find their way to a meaningful life if modern apostles spoke to them as Paul spoke to the people of Antioch. The gospel as Paul taught it has the power to transcend even the burden of poverty in the inner city. Paul saw among the poor the promise of a more fulfilled life, a member of the body of Christ capable of loving and being loved, and of serving others in the spirit of Jesus. It is this perception of goodness in the lives of the poor, regardless of how they appear to the eyes of a comfortable and satisfied middle class, that enables the apostle to bring a message of hope. An awareness of personal dignity is the beginning of a new life. We could well fall on our knees as Paul did on his, in wonderment that God has invited these people of little worldly privilege to be members of his own body, one with all others in Christ.

However, in our day, one step more is necessary, our exercise of advocacy for the poor, to fulfill our responsibility in the political order, to bring about the changes that are necessary if the poor in our inner cities are to live a life worthy of the children of God that they are. The scandal is that we already share the life of Christ together. We are all Christians. We are people of different races, different ethnic groups, different nationalities and backgrounds. Paul is telling us that these differences are not important. We must assert strongly the life of Christ that already binds us together and corrects the injustices, the segregation or discrimination which leaves the poor of the inner city in a disadvantaged state while the middle class enjoys the conveniences of our contemporary life.

"I have a great following in that city," God told Paul as he instructed him to stay in Corinth. God had a great following in Antioch, and Paul and the early preachers were able to see it, despite the hostility that may have existed, or the disdain of wealthy for poor, of conqueror for conquered, of free for slave. Likewise in our day, we must break through the bias and misconception of the poor, the black, the Hispanic, or other underprivileged groups in the inner city. By getting to know them better, becoming sensitive to the goodness hidden beneath customs and behavior that are strange to us, we may begin to see, as Paul saw in the people of Antioch, the potentiality of spiritual and religious growth, the capacity of becoming exemplary members of the body of Christ.

This is not easy. It requires effort; it requires preparation, instruction in the widespread knowledge we have today of culture, characteristics of culture and social class, skills of intercultural understanding and communication. Even more difficult, it requires an understanding of political and social processes to correct injustices that exist, and to make available to the poor of the inner city the opportunities for self-fulfillment and political participation in our great cities.

What made the difference in Paul, and what can make the difference in us, was his profund knowledge and love of Jesus. "Let this mind be in you which was in Christ Jesus," he prays in Philippians 2. "He did not see his godhead as something to cling to. He emptied himself to assume the condition of a slave." He did this to bring salvation to all. He broke down the enmity between Jew and Gentile, and his life became the basis of peace for all men and women. If that mind can be in us, it will be the inspiration to guide us to take the necessary steps to know and understand the poor of the inner city, and to open up the structures of our society so that the unity that binds us together in Jesus may express itself in our social life and enable us to find a way of breaking the barriers of prejudice, misunderstanding, and discrimination which separate us in the Antiochs of the modern world.

3. Thessalonica

After the harrowing experiences of imprisonment and earthquake at Philippi and the frenzied request of the authorities that they leave the place, Paul came to Thessalonica, a busy commercial center on the Bay of Thessalonica that leads into the Aegean Sea.

Thessalonica was an independent city; in other words, it had been granted autonomy by the Roman emperor because of the assistance it had offered to Rome in some of its military engagements. It was at the time of Paul, the largest city in Macedonia, "practically the capital of all Greece, Illyricum and Macedonia," as some scholars describe it. As a free city, it had no Roman soldiers, so different from Antioch, for example. This was the flourishing, busy, proud metropolis of the Roman world. (Cf. Otto F. A. Meinardus, *Saint Paul in Greece*, Athens: Lycabettus Press, 1973.)

Like most port cities in Greece at the time, it had the usual population of a commercial center. It was an active fishing center and every morning the fishermen could be seen drying and mending their nets as they still do after they had delivered their catch to the market. As a port city it was a center for longshoremen who handled the cargo and oxcarts that carried the cargo to and from the piers; it had warehouses, a financial center for the exchange of money and accounts of buyers and sellers. It had a population of Jews of the diaspora who had their own synagogue, and it had the wealthy and privileged families together with the servant population, most of whom were slaves. It was a typical city with its mixture of wealthy and poor, its natives and foreigners, its influential people who enjoyed power and those who were seeking it.

Into the midst of this hustling city, Paul arrived after his journey from Philippi. He set himself up as a tentmaker and set about earning his living at his trade. This must have brought him quickly into contact with other craftsmen (was he challenged as a new competitor?), with the markets where he had to purchase his materials and where he had to sell his finished products, and with the authorities of the city from whom he may have had to seek authorizations. In any event, in Thessalonica, Paul was a workingman among the others, earning his own livelihood by his trade and boastful that he was not a burden to the people of the city who befriended him.

> You know how you are supposed to imitate us; now we were not idle when we were with you, nor did we ever have our meals at anyone's table without paying for them; no, we worked night and day, slaving and straining so as not to be a burden to any of you. This was not because we had no right to be, but in order to make ourselves an example for you to follow (2 Thess 3:7–9).

Thus Paul was a workingman, "slaving and straining, day and night" as he put it. His was not a position among the affluent, but among the toiling artisans, eking out a livelihood by the work of his hands. He knew the world of work and struggle, of production and marketing, the uncertainties of trade and commerce, the trials of a small businessman's life. Not only did he know the inner city; in Thessalonica he was part of it.

As usual, Paul began his evangelizing effort in the synagogue of the Jews. For three weeks he spoke there proclaiming the gospel of Jesus. "Some of them were convinced and joined Paul and Silas, and so did many other God-fearing people and Greeks, as well as a number of rich women" (Acts 17:4). It appears that Paul was enjoying an initial success. The Jews were evidently merchants as they tended to be in the diaspora, skilled in the exchange of money and in matters of trade. They were evidently not among the very poor. It is interesting that Paul attracted some of the wealthy women. Who the God-fearing people were of the Greeks is not clear. But Paul's later experience reveals another aspect of life in Thessalonica.

"The Jews, full of resentment, enlisted the help of a gang from the marketplace, stirred up a crowd, and soon had the city in an uproar" (Acts 17:5). They could not find Paul since his friends were getting him secretly out of the city. But they created plenty of trouble for the families that had befriended Paul. Who were the thugs whom the opponents of Paul hired to attack him? Very likely the rough element found in so many port cities; tough, possibly unemployed seamen waiting for a ship or cast-offs of a crew. It suggests that, like so many modern cities, there was a pocket of violent young men, available, as in the instance of Paul, to do the dirty work of any person who chose to hire them.

What does this say about Paul and about Thessalonica? Like all Greek cities, a large segment of the population were slaves. Slavery in Roman cities was not similar to the slavery of blacks in the western world. Some of them were highly educated people who had lost their freedom in military conquests; others were artisans who served the wealthy families; others did the menial tasks of households or businesses. Paul was certainly in contact with all of these. Slaves constituted a segment of the early Christian communities, and repeatedly Paul writes to his fellow Christians emphatically reminding them that they are no longer "Jew or Greek, slave or free, male or female, but all of you are one in Christ Jesus" (Gal 3:28; 12:13). In his letter to Philemon, Paul reveals many aspects of the place of slaves in the Christian community. Onesimus was a runaway slave of Philemon, a friend of Paul's in Colossae. Paul makes no effort to gain freedom for Onesimus. Actually he is sending him back, but with the following words to Philemon:

> I know you have been deprived of Onesimus for a time, but it was only so that you would have him back forever, not as a slave any more, but something much better than a slave, a dear brother, especially dear to me, but how much more to you, as a blood brother as well as a brother in the Lord. So if all that we have in common means anything to you, welcome him as you would me; but if he has wronged you in any way or owes you anything, then let me pay for it (Phil 15–19).

Not all the slaves in Thessalonica would have been as close to Paul as Onesimus. But Paul would certainly have been in contact with them. They were not the "poor" population of a modern city. But they were people of limited political privileges and civil rights as we would describe them today. What Paul sought to give them was a sense of personal dignity as Christians, as brothers and sisters in the Lord. He advises Philemon to receive Onesimus as his brother in the Lord although

Onesimus is still his slave. Paul always insisted that brotherhood or sisterhood in the faith transcended social status.

> All baptized in Christ, you have all clothed yourself in Christ, and there are no distinctions between Jew and Greek, slave or free, male or female, but all of you are one in Christ Jesus (Gal 3:27–28).

What slaves failed to achieve in the political or social sphere, they achieved in the religious sphere in their consciousness of their unity in Jesus Christ.

Who were the others? Paul, in his first letter to the Thessalonians, is very critical of those who would not work. Idleness must have been a problem in Thessalonica since Paul makes so much of it. He urges them ". . . to go on making even greater progress, and to make a point of living quietly, attending to your own business and earning your living just as we told you to, so that you are seen to be respectable by those outside the church . . ." (1 Thess 4:10–12). In the second letter, he is even more emphatic: "In the name of the Lord Jesus Christ, we urge you, brothers, to keep away from any of the brothers who refuse to work or to live according to the tradition we passed on to you" (2 Thess 3:6). And it appears that Paul's work in Thessalonica was an effort to be a model of industriousness to them: "You know how you are supposed to imitate us; now we were not idle when we were with you . . ." (2 Thess 3:7).

> We gave you a rule when we were with you: not to let anyone have any food if he refused to do any work. Now we hear that there are some of

> you who are living in idleness, doing no work themselves but interfering with everyone else's. In the Lord Jesus Christ, we order and call on people of this kind to go on quietly working and earning the food they eat (2 Thess 3:10–12).

The unemployed must have been members of the church. Were they also a segment of a larger pocket of unemployed such as the thugs who were hired to do a job on Paul? Most commentators think that a strong belief that Christ would soon return developed in some of the Christians a disinterest in the things of the world, including work. It is obvious that if this was the case, Paul had no patience with the Christians who had given up work.

It is doubtful that Paul is referring to persons who were unemployed because they could not find work. If we can judge from conditions in Rome, unemployment among the very poor was very common. The emperors kept peace among the poor by offering "bread and circuses" and sought to avoid revolts by means of pacification. Paul was an artisan. He simply set up his own workshop or hired himself out to an employer; it is not clear. He would most likely have been concerned about the "unemployed poor" as we know them. He was evidently speaking to unemployed persons who, if they wished, could have found employment.

Working for one's living, then, was part of Paul's spiritual as well as practical teaching. And he spoke from his own experience. Paul was not a social activist or community organizer. But the gospel he preached had an extraordinary impact on wealthy and poor, a sense of personal dignity and importance as a member of the body of Christ. It was Paul's conviction that, if all lived as brothers and sisters in Christ, what we call social problems would begin to take care of themselves. The problem of sexual immorality must have been widespread in Thessalonica as it was in most Roman cities of that time. He speaks to them earnestly:

> What God wants is for all of you to be holy. He wants you to keep away from fornication, and each one of you to know how to use the body that belongs to him in a way that is holy and honorable, not giving way to selfish lust *like the pagans who do not know God* (1 Thess 4:3–5).

His success in Thessalonica was impressive. He praises them as ". . . the great example to all believers in Macedonia and Achaia, since it was from you that the word of the Lord started to spread." They were mostly Gentiles who suffered from the hostility of the Jews because they followed Paul and accepted his teaching. Undiscouraged by the immorality, by the hostility of the Jews, by the hoodlums, or by the laziness of some of his followers who expected the second coming at any moment, he found in these people a response to the good news of Jesus Christ. In the inner city of Thessalonica, another of the great Christian communities began to come alive.

4. Corinth

After a discouraging visit to Athens, the intellectual and cultural center of the Greek world, Paul set out for the tough and turbulent port city of Corinth. Paul never went back to Athens. He had little reason to expect much more in Corinth, a very busy center of trade and shipping, a key point in the communications system of the Roman legions. Corinth was a mixture of people from many parts of the world. It was also the capital of the Roman province of Achaia. It had some of the characteristics of Antioch; it was big, important, active, cosmopolitan, but it lacked the beauty and culture that lent some balance to life in Antioch. It was well known for the temple prostitutes who plied their trade on the mountain that towered over the city. "Corinthian girl" became the nickname for a prostitute. Corinth was notorious for its immorality. It was a center of games, and it was in his letters to the Corinthians that Paul used the examples from athletic competition. It was a center also of theatrical performances; its theater numbered three thousand seats, and it had a music hall which held an audience of eighteen hundred. Here were the wealthy and the influential; but crowded into the city were the poor, the seamen, longshoremen, draymen, thousands of menial workers and slaves, often oppressed and overworked, the people of the inner city.

What may have attracted Paul was the large Jewish population in the city. These were merchants who were active in trade, but they were joined by many more who had been driven out of Rome a few years earlier by the persecution of Emperor Claudius. Among these were two of the first acquaintances Paul made, Aquila and Priscilla, a husband and wife who were to become two of the most outstanding figures in the early church. They were also tentmakers. Paul not only lodged with them, but set up shop with them as a tentmaker.

Paul's success was immediate and something of a sensation. He preached to the Jews that Jesus was the messiah. Many believed in Jesus as a result of his preaching, including the president of the synagogue and his whole household. Eventually, the unbelieving Jews turned against him; he shook the dust of his cloak out against them and turned to an apostolate among the pagans.

It appears that Paul was frightened in Corinth—one of the few moments when fear is mentioned in Paul's life. The Lord appeared to him in a vision and spoke to him: "Do not be afraid to speak out, nor allow yourself to be silenced; I am with you; I have so many people on my side in that city that no one will ever attempt to hurt you" (Acts 18:9–10). Paul stayed, and out of this unpromising crowd of people he was able to develop one of the great congregations of the early church.

Paul again refers to fear when he asks the Corinthians to be good to Timothy: "If Timothy comes, show him that he has nothing to be afraid of in you; like me he is doing the Lord's work, and no one should be scornful of him" (1 Cor 16:10).

Again we are with Paul in the inner city, in the midst of the dust and dirt, the animals and carts, merchants and tradesmen, workers and slaves, actors and athletes, soldiers going to foreign lands or returning, thousands hustling for a few coins, a little recognition or prominence, a touch of political power. What a time

Paul was to have with them! Look at the way he describes them in his first letter to them:

> Take yourselves, for instance, brothers, at the time when you were called: how many of you were wise in the ordinary sense of the word; how many were influential people, or came from noble families? No, it was to shame the wise that God chose what is foolish by human reckoning, and to shame what is strong that he chose what is weak by human reckoning; those whom the world thinks common and contemptible are the ones God has chosen—those who are nothing at all to show up those who are everything.

The "nobodies" of Corinth, the common people held in contempt by the respectable citizens, the people of the inner city; how similar to the attitude today of the respectable middle class toward the poor and helpless of what we call our "slums." These were the ones God was referring to in his vision to Paul: "I have a great following in that city; don't be afraid." And Paul, referring to their remarkable spiritual growth, was able to say to them at the beginning of his letter:

> I never stop thanking God for all the graces you have received through Jesus Christ. I thank him that you have been enriched in so many ways, especially in your teachers and preachers; the witness of Christ has indeed been strong among you (1:4–6).

The achievement was great. As Paul keeps saying, "It was God who gave the increase." But scattered throughout the letter is the evidence of the troubles he had.

> Brothers, I was unable to speak to you as people of the Spirit; I treated you as sensual men, still infants in Christ. What I fed you with was milk, not solid food, for you were not ready for it, and, indeed, you are still not ready for it, since you are still unspiritual. Isn't that obvious from all the jealousy and wrangling there is among you, from the way you go on behaving like ordinary people? (3:1–3).

And what was the price Paul was paying?

> To this day we go without food and drink and clothes; we are beaten and have no homes; we work for our living with our own hands. When we are cursed, we answer with a blessing; when we are wounded, we put up with it; when we are insulted, we answer politely; we are treated as the offal of the world, still to this day, the scum of the earth (4:11–13).

Paul's letter reflects not only the troubles he had with the Christian community, but the troubles the community itself had in the experience of living in a pagan world. Immorality was prevalent in Corinth, and Paul was realistic in counseling his people. Among Christians, immorality was not to be tolerated. He was severe in his counsel—too severe it appears to people of our day. But, in the circumstances of Corinth, Paul must have been convinced that this was the only way to maintain a genuinely Christian community. However, he realized that Christians could not wall themselves up in an isolated community.

> When I wrote in my letter to you not to associate with people living immoral lives, I was not meaning to include all the people in the world who are sexually immoral, any more than I meant to include all usurers and swindlers or idol worshipers. To do that you would have to withdraw from the world altogether (1 Cor 5:9–11).

One gets a glimpse of the pervasiveness of evil in the city as Christians saw it. Paul was in no way as tolerant with Christians.

> What I wrote was that you should not associate with a brother Christian who is leading an immoral life, or is a usurer, or idolatrous, or a slanderer, or a drunkard or is dishonest; you should not even eat a meal with people like that (5:11).

And, with reference to a man accused of incest, Paul was adamant: "You must drive out this evil-doer from among you" (5:13).

How should a Christian relate to the evil in the world? This is a more challenging problem in our day than it was in Paul's. Evil in Paul's day was much more personal; it was the particular loan shark who practically enslaved his debtors; it was a particular farmer who exploited his tenants; it was a particular slave-owner who abused his slaves. They knew who the evil-doer was and they could drive him out. Today many of the evils are institutionalized: they result from the functioning of massive economic or political institutions. People are homeless in New York City not only because a particular exploiting landlord put his tenants out; it is also a result of the decisions of the federal government not to provide funds for housing for the poor; of changes in the stock market far removed from the poor families who lose their homes in the process and far beyond their power to control them; of the rapid changes in modern city neighborhoods which the poor are helpless to prevent. The poor are unemployed not only because one employer refused to give them work; it is often the result of vast technological changes and automation that replace workers by machines, or the complications of international trade, one nation selling more cheaply than another. A response to this requires a type of organized political action that was unknown in Paul's day.

However, that is not the only way evil is present in the inner city of today. The poor do know who the petty drug pushers are—another problem that Paul did not have to face; they know the alcoholics whose problems we understand much better than Paul ever did; they know the loan sharks who exploit them as they did in Paul's day; there are persons with whom they can refuse to eat, and whom they could dismiss from the congregation. It is not likely that the evil-doers would be members of the inner city parish, and the poor are more concerned about protecting themselves against the evildoers than dismissing them from the Christian community.

But the problem of relating to the evil of the world remains, and Paul's firmness is a method that is used only with great caution today. Paul's counsel reflects the radical commitment that a Christian had to make in those days to be faithful to Jesus. Without such intense loyalty to the Christian community, its survival would have been impossible.

In the inner city of the present day, however, practically everyone is a baptized Christian, unevangelized, in most cases with little instruction in the faith, with shreds of folk religious practices as a frail link to the Lord, and caught in the turmoil for survival. Thus the scene is different. It is not a pagan world that has never heard of Jesus; it is a Christian world that has lost its inner life, or has never had the benefit of a strong religious development. Therefore, to follow Paul's counsel to his followers, "Have nothing to do with the Christians who are evil-doers," must be related to our contemporary situation where all the evil-doers are nominally Christians. The cultivation of a strong sense of community among the faithful is essential. The "basic Christian communities" of Central and South America are a model to be followed. They give to the faithful Christians a deep sense of identity and solidarity, a confidence in the support of brothers and sisters in the presence of confusion, conflict and neighborhood violence.

A strong small Christian community would not only serve to encourage faithful Christians in their service of God; it would be a source of inspiration and motivation for the service of one's neighbor that is necessary for the protection of people in the inner city today. The experience of the small Christian community, the reflection on the scriptures, the mutual support of a life of service and sacrifice for others, could result in the kinds of community action which are necessary if the innocent poor are to have the capacity to protect themselves against the drugs, the loan sharks, the pimps, the thieves of the inner city. It will also motivate them in the more complicated forms of organization they need to cope with the failure of public and private institutions to provide for the well-being of the community. The deeply committed community of the faithful in Paul's time was the great source of protection against the impact of the evils of the pagan world; a similar deeply committed community of faithful in the inner city of today could be the source of protection against the impact of the evils of a modern Christian world that has in many ways become corrupt.

The same inspiration must be kept alive. "I have a great following in that city, Paul; do not be afraid." Jesus has a great following as well in the inner cities of today, if modern apostles will search them out, look for the seeds of spiritual greatness, and bring the life and word of Jesus to the poor who hunger for them. This is where Paul becomes the impressive role model. He never lost heart; he searched tirelessly for ". . . all that rings true, all that makes for right, all that is lovely in the telling; virtue and merit wherever virtue and merit can be found" (Phil 4:8). If these are foremost in our minds, we will find them in the lives of the inner city poor, and the hope that Paul found in the Corinthians may be found in the inner cities of today.

Order Versus Disorder

Paul had a difficult time with his Corinthians. This was no overnight conversion. They were not models of Christian courtesy and restraint to begin with. They were a disorderly, thoughtless and selfish group. Exhorting them to a virtuous life, Paul describes some of them:

> You know perfectly well that people who do wrong will not inherit the kingdom of God: peo-

> ple of immoral lives, idolators, catamites, sodomites, thieves, usurers, drunkards, slanderers, and swindlers will never inherit the kingdom of God. *These are the sort of people some of you once were*, but now you have been washed clean (1 Cor 6:9–11). (Italics mine.)

And Paul is critical of their assemblies when they gather to eat before celebrating the eucharist:

> I cannot say that you have done well in holding meetings that do more harm than good. In the first place, I hear that, when you all come together as a community, there are separate factions among you, and I half believe it—since there must no doubt be separate groups among you, to distinguish those who are to be trusted. The point is, when you hold these meetings, it is not the Lord's supper that you are eating, since, when the time comes to eat, everyone is in such a hurry to start his own supper that one person goes hungry while another is getting drunk. Surely you have homes for eating and drinking in? Surely you have enough respect for the community of God not to make the poor people embarrassed? What am I to say to you? Congratulate you? I cannot congratulate you on this (1 Cor 11:17–22).

Problems of the rich and poor appear here: the wealthy who have plenty to eat, and who evidently make a show of it, while the poor go hungry. Paul advises the affluent to eat at home before they come to the meal with the assembly. In this way the differences between those who have and those who have not will not be a point of division or embarrassment, and the occasion for disorder at the meeting will be eliminated.

Quite apart from the meals, Paul had problems keeping order in the assemblies:

> At all your meetings, let everyone be ready with a psalm or a sermon or a revelation, or ready to use his gift of tongues or to give an interpretation; but it must be done for the common good. If there are people present with the gift of tongues, let only two or three at the most be allowed to use it, and only one at a time, and there must be someone to interpret. If there is no interpreter present, they must keep quiet in church and speak only to themselves and God. As for prophets, let two or three of them speak and others attend to them . . . prophets can always control their prophetic spirits, since God is not a God of disorder but of peace (1 Cor 14:26–32).

One gets the impression of everyone trying to speak at the same time, everyone with his little prophecy, or prayer, or speaking in tongues, and Paul trying to keep some order in the meeting. "God is the God of peace, not disorder." It also appears that the women may have tried to get into the act, a violation of expected behavior of women in church, a heritage of the long tradition of the Jewish temple and synagogues. "Women are to remain quiet at meetings since they have no permission to speak; they must keep in the background as the law lays it down" (1 Cor 14:34).

Meantime Paul was teaching them of the true mystery of the resurrection of Jesus and the hope of our own resurrection; and he makes the remarkable statement on love in 1 Corinthians 13:1–13: "If I speak with the eloquence of men and of angels, but speak without love, I am simply a gong booming or a cymbal clashing. . . ." His first letter to the Corinthians contains some of the great passages in Christian literature, and statements of Christian belief and practice that have guided the church since Paul's time.

It was in his first letter to the Corinthians that the first written statement of the eucharist appears:

> For this is what I received from the Lord, and in turn passed on to you: that on the same night that he was betrayed, the Lord Jesus took some bread, and thanked God for it and broke it, and he said, "This is my body which is for you, do this as a memorial of me." In the same way he took the cup after supper and said, "This cup is the new covenant in my blood, Whenever you drink it, do it as a memorial of me" (1 Cor 11:23–26).

Paul instructs the Corinthians carefully about the celebration of the eucharist. It appears that he had a hard time with some of them. His language suggests that some of them may have died as a punishment for their irreverence.

> Until the Lord comes, therefore, every time you eat this bread and drink this cup, you are proclaiming his death, and so any one who eats the bread or drinks the cup of the Lord unworthily will be behaving unworthily toward the body and blood of the Lord.

> Everyone is to recollect himself before eating this bread and drinking this cup, because a person who eats and drinks without recognizing the body is eating and drinking to his own condemnation. In fact, that is why many of you are weak and ill and some of you have died. If only we recollected ourselves we should not be punished like that. But when the Lord does punish like that it is to correct us and stop us from being condemned with the world (1 Cor 11:28–32).

And central to Paul's teaching was, of course, the resurrection. Here again there appears to have been resistance to his teaching. He insists on the importance of this central mystery:

> And if Christ raised from the dead is what has been preached, how can some of you be saying that there is no resurrection of the dead? If there is no resurrection of the dead, Christ himself cannot have been raised, and if Christ has not been raised, then our preaching is useless and your believing is useless; indeed we are shown up as witnesses who have committed perjury before God, because we swore in evidence before God that he had raised Christ to life. For, if the dead are not raised, Christ has not been raised, and if Christ has not been raised, you are still in your sins, and what is more serious, all who have died in Christ have perished. If our hope in Christ has been for this life only, we are the most unfortunate of people.
>
> But Christ has in fact been raised from the dead, the first fruits of all who have fallen

> asleep. Death came through one man, and in the same way the resurrection of the dead has come through one man. Just as all men died in Adam, so all men will be brought to life in Christ (1 Cor 15:12–22).

Paul said that he was giving the Corinthians spiritual "baby food" as it were. But it is clear that he was emphasizing the basic truths of the faith, strongly and clearly; and his statements constitute the teachings that the most sophisticated Christians have used over the centuries. This suggests to us that, in dealing with inner city people, this basic doctrine, taught clearly and emphatically, will be as effective in our day as it was in Paul's.

The significance of this teaching is all the more impressive in view of the moral and spiritual problems that Corinth posed for the early Christians. Fornication was common in Corinth, and Paul's condemnation of it (1 Cor 6:12–20) is emphatic and clear. "Keep away from fornication. All other sins are committed outside the body; but to fornicate is to sin against your own body."

Living in a Pagan World

With all his vigorous pronouncements, Paul manifests remarkable understanding and compassion in his pastoral advice to Christians about living in the pagan world. The problem was not so much the worship of idols and pagan gods. He taught that Christians must not participate in the sacrifices in the pagan temples. Paul was emphatic on that. The pastoral problem was posed by the food that was purchased in the market. Paul told Christians not to worry about whether it had been sacrificed or not. And when Christians were invited to the homes of pagans he advised them: ". . . eat whatever is put before you without asking questions just to satisfy conscience" (1 Cor 10:27). Paul knew the aggravations of trying to determine what had or had not been sacrificed; he also appreciated the embarrassment that would ensue if Christians kept questioning pagan friends and neighbors about the food. There was a decidedly practical aspect to his pastoral guidance. Paul told the Christians to eat what was served. However, Paul was concerned with the sensitive conscience of more scrupulous Christians. If a scrupulous Christian did raise the question at a meal at a pagan's home and was told that the food had been sacrificed to idols, he suggested that it would be charitable for the other Christians not to eat it "for the sake of his scruples—his scruples, you see, not your own." Paul was concerned about the need of the Christians to live in a pagan world; he did not want them to be hermits or to segregate themselves. He knew the problems this created for Christians. He sought to give them moral guidance that would protect their conscience but enable them to live with pagan neighbors. Paul was sensitive to the differing cultures of the Gentile world. He was clear and decisive about the essentials of Christian faith and morality; his firm assertions about the immorality of fornication, usury, slander, and drunkenness were evidence of this. Nevertheless, he saw the need to be accommodating on the issue of food and in the situation of Christians married to a pagan spouse (if the pagan objected, he said, the Christian spouse could terminate the marriage and marry a Christian). He was also aware of the role of the father in selecting a husband for his daughter. He was not very concerned about the civil status of slaves (slaves, as we have seen, were not like the slaves of the United States; many of them were really persons of skill and ability, but without the civil rights of free Roman citizens). "If, when you were called, you were a slave, do not let this bother you; but if you should have the chance of being free, accept it" (1 Cor 8:21). Paul was so enthralled by the freedom all Christians had in Christ that the particular status of a person in society was of less concern to him.

Continuing Discouragement

The second letter to the Corinthians adds further evidence of the difficulties Paul faced among the Corinthians. After a beautiful opening that is now used at the beginning of the Liturgy of Christian Burial ("Blessed be the God and Father of our Lord Jesus Christ, a gentle Father and the God of all consolation . . ."), and after recalling the threats to his life in Asia, he brings up the difficulties with the Corinthians:

> By my life, I call God to witness that the reason why I did not come to Corinth after all was to spare your feelings. We are not dictators over your faith, but are fellow workers with you for your happiness; in the faith you are steady enough. Well then, I made up my mind not to pay you a second distressing visit. I may have hurt you but if so I have hurt the only people who could give me any pleasure. . . . When I wrote to you in deep distress and anguish of mind and in tears, it was not to make you feel hurt but to let you know how much love I have for you (2 Cor 2:1–4).

All through the letter there are suggestions of criticism against Paul, opposition, misrepresentation, failure to reform their lives. Some criticized him for being gentle when he was with them, but tough in his letters: "I am the man who is so humble when he is facing you, but bullies you at a distance" (2 Cor 10:1). "Someone said: 'He writes powerful and strongly-worded letters, but when he is with you, you see only half a man and no preacher at all'" (10:10). Although they criticized Paul, they were ready to listen to every new doctrine that anyone preached.

> But the serpent, with his cunning, seduced Eve, and I am afraid that, in the same way, your ideas may get corrupted and turned away from simple devotion to Christ, because any newcomer has only to proclaim a new Jesus, different from the one that we preached, or you have only to receive a new spirit, different from the one you have already received, or a new gospel, different from the one you have already accepted—and you welcome it with open arms (11:3–6).

They even criticized him for earning his own living, or for being supported by Christians from Macedonia. "I was very careful, and I always shall be, not to be a burden to you in any way" (10:9–10). Paul then offers his own boast:

> Hebrews are they? So am I. Israelites? So am I. Descendants of Abraham? So am I. The servants of Christ? I must be mad to say this, but so am I, and more than they (2 Cor 1:22–23).

Paul then goes on to list his labors and sufferings for the gospel, boasting only in the Lord, as he says:

> So I shall be very happy to make my weaknesses my special boast so that the power of

> Christ may stay over me, and that is why I am quite content with my weaknesses, and with insults, hardships, persecutions, and the agonies I go through for Christ's sake. For it is when I am weak that I am strong (2 Cor 12:9–10).

He then comes to that sad ending of his letter that reveals the disappointments, frustrations, and problems he had with the people of Corinth:

> What I am afraid of is that when I come I may find you different from what I want you to be, and you may find that I am not as you would like me to be; and then there will be wrangling, jealousy, and tempers roused, intrigues, and backbiting and gossip, obstinacies and disorder. I am afraid that, on my next visit, my God may make me ashamed on your account and I shall be grieving over all those who have sinned before and have still not repented of the impurities, fornication and debauchery they committed (2 Cor 12:20–21).

But Paul never gave up on the Corinthians. As he told them at the beginning of his letter:

> There is one thing we are proud of, and our conscience tells us that it is true: that we have always treated everybody, and especially you, with the reverence and sincerity which come from God, and, by the grace of God, we have done this without any ulterior motives. There are no hidden meanings in our letters besides what you can read for yourselves and under-

> stand. And I hope that, although you do not know us very well yet, you will have come to recognize, when the day of our Lord Jesus comes, that you can be as proud of us as we are of you (2 Cor 1:12–14).

He treated them "with reverence and sincerity," looking forward to the day when he would be proud of them, as they would be of him. He never tired of searching out in them ". . . all that is right, all that is good, all that is lovely in the telling, virtue and merit wherever virtue and merit may be found." There among the people whom the world despised, who gave him endless grief and troubles and reason to weep, Paul never gave up. Eventually the good that was hidden beneath the disorder, the sin, the complaints, the criticism, began to emerge and the greatness of the Corinthian church began to manifest itself.

This is really the lesson of Paul among the Corinthians. How do you deal with people of the inner city? "With reverence and sincerity," trusting in God to use our weakness to reveal his own strength through us, and never giving in to discouragement. "Do not be afraid, Paul. I have so many people on my side in that city that no one will ever attempt to hurt you" (Acts 18:10).

And, of course, Paul never fails to make his collection for the suffering in Jerusalem. He reminds them of the great generosity of the Macedonians who gave so much even though they were poor themselves. "I can swear that they gave not only as much as they could afford, but far more, and quite spontaneously" (2 Cor 8:3). Paul reminds them of their own generous spirit: "You always have the most of everything—of faith, of eloquence, of understanding, of keenness for any cause, and the biggest share of our affection—so we expect you to put the most into this work of mercy too" (8:7). Paul praises them for having started the collection the previous year. He now asks them to finish it.

The Corinthians had evidently been most generous. Paul even cautions them not to give beyond their means. "This does not mean that to give relief to others you ought to make things difficult for yourselves; it is a question of balancing what happens to be your surplus now against their present need" (2 Cor 8:13).

Everyone who has worked with inner city people remarks how generous they can be with one another. Once it becomes clear that someone is in real need, they respond. This was evident in all the cities where Paul evangelized. He never forgot the needs of the church in Jerusalem. And the Christians of the inner city, many of them poor, gave generously for their brothers and sisters in Jerusalem.

Thus the effort of Paul continues, and the reverence and respect he had for the Corinthians bore fruit in the strength of the great church at Corinth. By imitating him, especially his patience, his endurance, his respect, his fearless presentation of the complete Christian life, it is possible that by our efforts the people of our own inner cities may be capable of the same achievement.

5. Jerusalem

Suffering: The Cost of Apostleship

Jerusalem was the city of Paul's constant concern; it was also the city of much of his suffering. Our first knowledge of Paul is his collaboration in Jerusalem with those who stoned Saint Stephen to death; near the end of his life Paul almost perished by the same method he once helped to visit on others.

Paul spent none of his time as an apostle in Jerusalem; therefore our reflection on his relation to Jerusalem is different from that of the other cities. One thing we know about the Christian community in Jerusalem: it was poor and constantly in need. Paul was always raising money to be sent for the relief of the poor in Jerusalem.

After his conversion Paul went to Jerusalem to spend some time with Peter. In the year 44 A.D., Paul came again with Barnabas to bring the money which the Christians in Antioch had donated for the victims of the famine in Jerusalem (Acts 11:27–30). He went to the Council of Jerusalem (Acts 15) to represent the cause of the Gentile Christians. The next we hear of him was his return to Jerusalem after his missionary journeys (Acts 21:15–26:32) where he nearly met death at the hands of the Jewish zealots.

Jerusalem

Jerusalem was the sacred city of the Jews. Here, on the great height of the city, was the magnificent center of Jewish religious life, the temple and its surrounding areas. Here was the holy of holies, carefully enshrined according to the dictates of the Mosaic law, and served by the class of priests to which Zechariah, father of John the Baptist, belonged. Here the people prayed daily, like Simeon who waited daily to see the day of the messiah, and like Anna the prophetess who never left the women's section of the temple where, in fasting and prayer, she waited for the deliverance of Jerusalem. How many thousands like them must have been found every day in the huge inner hall of the temple? Jesus most certainly became one of them on his visits to Jerusalem. It was here that he was presented to the temple, and it was here as a boy of twelve that he visited with Mary and Joseph and where they found him, staying behind, and in discussion with the priests. This was the focus of that which was most holy in Jewish life.

Outside the temple and surrounding it at a lower level was the enormous expanse of the court of the Gentiles. Here was the confusion and noise of thousands of animals destined for slaughter for sacrifices which Jews were obliged to make yearly; here were the money changers exchanging foreign coins for the temple currency which alone could be used for the payment of the temple tax. It was a scene of turbulence, of business transactions, of the sounds of animals, the shouts and conversations of thousands gathered there. One can imagine the intensity of human interaction in this center of Jewish religious, social and economic life. Here Jesus drove the buyers and sellers out of the courtyard because they had made the house of his Father a "den of thieves."

Near the temple was the other presence, the fortress of the Roman governor and of the Roman army of occupation. The Roman presence was evident in the Roman legionnaires, the military power assuring the preservation of order and the protection of the vested interests of wealthy priests and businessmen against the dangers of insurrection. There were the satellites of the occupying power, the hated publicans or tax collectors. John the Baptist told them, "Exact no more than your rate" (Lk 3:13). That was not an effective lesson; they exploited the people for their own petty profit.

There was the religious establishment: the high priests profiting from the concessions to merchants in the temple court, the scribes, the Pharisees, the array of functionaries at various levels of administration of the law. Jesus confronted them with a surprising fierceness of language.

There were the merchants, large and small, thousands of them along the narrow streets, selling their wares. There were the poor of every large city, the sick who rushed to seek a cure at the pool of Bethsaida, the lepers in their isolated enclaves observing their required distance from the busy world that rushed around them. There were the artisans whose skills enabled the city to function, the servants and menial workers, the unemployed that Jesus must have been looking at when he taught with his parable of the workers hired at different times of the day. These were the tumultuous crowds that must have greeted Jesus at his entry into Jerusalem.

Then there were the omnipresent insurrectionists who were organizing military strength to drive the Romans out of Palestine. Simon, one of the apostles, had been a zealot; Barabbas, chosen for liberation in preference to Jesus, had murdered a man in an insurrection. The tribune who arrested Paul (Acts 21:38) thought he was the Egyptian who had started a recent riot in the city. Intermingled in all of these were the zealots for the law, the traditions of Moses. Some of them had followed

Paul from the cities of Asia Minor and stirred the crowds of Jerusalem against him. It was only the intervention of the Roman legionnaires that saved him. His Roman citizenship was his claim to protection and the judicial process.

This was the Jerusalem to which Paul had returned, bringing the money he had collected from the Gentile Christians for the relief of the poor in Jerusalem.

The lessons of Paul's experience in Jerusalem are not the same as that of his experience in evangelizing the poor in Antioch, Thessalonica or Corinth. But there are lessons to be learned. Paul had gone to extraordinary lengths to raise money for the poor Jewish Christians in Jerusalem. During the great famine of 44 A.D., the Christians of Antioch sent a contribution of money to the Christians of Jerusalem. Paul himself brought this and gave it to the elders for distribution (Acts 11:29–30). There was his great praise for the generosity of the church of Macedonia: ". . . throughout great trials and suffering, their constant cheerfulness and their intense poverty have overflowed in a wealth of generosity" (2 Cor 8:1–2). And he begs the Corinthians to be equally generous: ". . . we expect you to put the most into this work of mercy also" (2 Cor 8:7).

When Paul arrived in Jerusalem, he had the revenues of these generous collections; he gave them to the "elders" of the church to be distributed. There is no indication in Acts 21:15–26 that the elders thanked Paul. They were too preoccupied with their own concerns about the preservation of the Mosaic law. Despite Paul's eloquent description of the remarkable spread of the church among the Gentiles, their evident hasty response was their questioning him about rumors that he was disregarding the law. They even subjected him to a test of his Jewishness, joining four nazirites in a purification ceremony that was long (seven days), very costly, and possibly harmful to the Gentile church, i.e., would the Gentiles interpret Paul's action as a weakening of his insistence on the freedom of the Gentiles from the Mosaic law?

The point here is that for all of Paul's great efforts to collect funds for the Jewish Christians in Jerusalem, and the great generosity of the Gentile churches, all Paul seemed to get was a test of his fidelity to the Mosaic law. And Paul, in a more than generous gesture, accepted it although it almost got him killed. What Paul's behavior is telling us is: Do not expect a reward in this world for generous service to the poor—especially if service of the poor must be channeled through official bureaucracies.

It must have been clear to Paul that, in Jerusalem, he was not only in a Jewish world that was passing; he was in the midst of a Christian community, closed, narrow, self-protective, that could not survive. They had none of that greatness of vision that had driven Paul: ". . . neither Jew nor Gentile, neither Greek nor Roman, neither slave nor free, but only Christ Jesus." When Paul came at great risk to Jerusalem, bursting with enthusiasm about the remarkable Gentile churches throughout the Greek and Roman world, he is seen only in terms of his possible threat to the law and the Mosaic tradition to which the Jerusalem Christians were dedicated. "Prove to us that you are really a Jew!" seemed to be the spirit of those who subjected him to the test of the vow.

The Christians at least did him no harm. It was the zealots of the law who seized him and sought to kill him. They accused him erroneously of profaning the temple by bringing a Gentile into it. They demanded his death because they claimed he was an enemy to the traditions of the Jews. Twice they rushed upon him threatening to tear him apart; forty of them formed a conspiracy not to eat or drink until they had killed him, a conspiracy that was overcome by the report of Paul's nephew to the tribune. It was only the alertness of the Roman army that eventually rescued him. The Jews were eventually to destroy themselves. Four thousand insurgents had been defeated in a recent revolt. They were to continue to rise up against the Roman occupation until Rome unleashed its fury upon them and destroyed their sacred city in the year 72 A.D.

The experience of Paul at Jerusalem is filled with meaning in relation to the apostolate to the inner cities of our own day. More than ever is there a need of apostles who become thoroughly familiar with the lives of the poor, and who can perceive as did Paul the values that are often obscured by forms of behavior which puzzle the more sophisticated middle class. Beneath the problems of drug addiction and alcoholism, of teenage pregnancies and female-headed households, of unemployment and public welfare, values can still be perceived which hold the promise of religious and spiritual development. But if the church becomes rigid, self-protective, and isolated, it will not have the capacity to open its arms for millions who are searching for the meaning of life which the church can give them. If, like the church of Jerusalem, it clings to the conventions and traditions of the past and thinks fearfully only of its own security, it will not be prepared to open itself to a population which, like the people of Corinth, may be the church of the future.

Serious questions like the ones that Paul faced must also be faced in the inner city apostolate. Which forms of behavior are compatible with the life and teaching of

Jesus, and which are not? Paul had to advise his converts about purchasing meat in the public markets. Had the meat been sacrificed to the idols? If you are a guest in someone's home and you think the meat for the meal was offered to the idols, what do you do? Don't do anything, advised Paul. No need to become involved in that kind of inquiry. And so today, we are faced with the new roles of women, new structures of family life, what behavior is "Christian" in a consumer society, what responsibilities we have to the homeless, the unemployed, the drop-outs or the pushed-out from our societies. In this new and complicated world, how can people express in their lives the spirit and truth of Jesus?

And the zealots are here as well. A challenge to the evils and injustice of that inner city may stir up the latent zealotry ready to erupt when interests or power are endangered. There is no Roman army of occupation, but the players in the inner city are just as well armed—seventy homicides among drug peddlers in the single month of July 1988 in New York City. An apostle challenges that kind of zealotry at his peril. Bringing the homeless into your home may cause it to be fire-bombed by respectable citizens who claim to be Christian. The zealots are not likely to tear you apart because of your religious beliefs, but their interests may be just as fiercely defended. Thus there is not only the loss of prestige and privilege; the physical danger is there as well. Paul tells us: do not be afraid. The Lord has a great following in the inner city. Do not be afraid.

The Primacy of Power

One other lesson about the inner city appears clearly in the experience of Paul. He was saved because, as a Roman citizen, he had the privilege of the protection of the law. The Roman army rescued him, and the Roman soldiers responded with complete restraint once they learned that Paul enjoyed the rights of a Roman citizen. Non-Romans were not so fortunate. The privilege of power did not extend to the religious beliefs and interests of those who were not Roman.

Roman officials were constantly bewildered when they came face to face with questions of religious differences and conflicts of religious interests. They did not want to be bothered by them. When Paul was brought before the tribunal in Corinth, Gallio, the Roman official, threw the accusers out: "Gallio said to the Jews: 'Listen, you Jews, if this were a misdemeanor or a crime, I would not hesitate to attend to you; but if it is only quibbles about words and names, and about your own law, then you must deal with it yourselves. I have no intention of making legal decisions about things like that'" (Acts 18:14–15). When Gallio sent them out of court, they ". . . turned on Sosthenes, the synagogue president, and beat him in front of the courthouse. Gallio refused to take any notice at all." Had Sosthenes been a Roman citizen, it would have been otherwise. Sosthenes did not enjoy the privilege of power.

This was the discriminatory application of Roman law: citizens are protected; non-citizens are punished. But when the Roman citizens became Christians and challenged the law that required religious adulation of the emperors, the protection of the law ended. Roman religious interests were to have the full protection of the law; Christian religious interests were to enjoy none.

Paul was kept in prison in Caesarea for two years, the limit that was permitted under Roman law for a prisoner who had not been convicted. Because of the determination of the Jewish zealots to kill him, Paul appealed to Caesar. He was sent to Rome under guard in a journey that was troubled with storms and shipwreck. But he arrived in Rome where he was kept in a form of house arrest. Anyone who wished to see him could come to him. He continued to instruct the Christians in Rome; he met with the Jews who showed none of the murderous hostility of the Jews in Jerusalem. Paul spoke to them repeatedly of Jesus and the fulfillment of the prophecies in the resurrection of Jesus. Some became Christians; others did not. Again, after another limit of two years of imprisonment, Paul was set free. It appears that he went on another long apostolic journey to the east and then returned to Rome where he was arrested again in the persecution of Nero. He was martyred in the year 67 A.D. More will be said about Rome later.

The Jews, who had murdered the prophets and demanded the crucifixion of Christ, did everything possible to do away with Paul as well. But Paul never allowed their hostility to diminish his love for them. They were the chosen people of the Lord. Paul wrote those strange words in his letter to the Romans: "What I want to say now is no pretense. I say it in union with Christ—it is the truth; my consicience in union with the Holy Spirit assures me of it too. What I want to say is this: my sorrow is so great, my mental anguish so endless, I would willingly be condemned and be cut off from Christ if it would help my brothers of Israel, my own flesh and blood" (Rom 9:1–4).

All the ungratefulness, all the violence and hostility notwithstanding, the profound love of Paul for his Jewish people still remains. He preached and taught and suffered to bring the gospel to them. When they refused, he did not reject them, but hoped that in his love for them, they would finally accept Jesus as their savior. There was no limit to the suffering he would endure for their salvation. No matter how great the trials and difficulties of the apostolate of the inner city, it never places on us the limit of suffering that Paul was willing to accept. "Don't ever be afraid," he would tell us. "Don't ever be afraid."

6. Rome

Paul did not travel to Rome to minister to its people. He came as a prisoner to appeal his cause to the emperor that he was not guilty of the crimes alleged against him by his enemies in Jerusalem. His first experience in Rome was as a prisoner confined to his lodging under house arrest. This lasted for two years. His second experience in Rome was his arrival again as a prisoner, condemned to death as a Christian in the persecution of Emperor Nero. Nevertheless in the two years of his first visit, Paul established contact with a wide range of people residing in Rome. It reflects the character of the city and the character of Paul. What was Rome like in the years 62–64 and how did Paul relate to this?

Rome

Paul arrived in Rome in the year 62, when Nero was the reigning emperor. Historically, Nero remains one of the worst examples in history of political madness and corruption. He had his own mother, Agrippina, murdered. She had maneuvered to get him on the throne in preference to Britannicus, the natural son of Emperor Claudius and the heir apparent. Nero later had his first wife, Octavia, murdered, and when there was some slight evidence that Britannicus was seeking the throne, Nero had him executed also. Reliable historians describe him as a disgrace to the empire. Tacitus, the great Roman historian, never mentions his name. He became emperor at the age of seventeen in the year 54, and committed suicide in 68 when it was clear he had lost all support of the army, the senate and the influential political leaders. Meanwhile he had manipulated to have the city burned in one of the great conflagrations of history, and then blamed it on the Christians, large numbers of whom he put to death in the brutalities of the Colosseum or by crucifixion. Peter, a Jew, was crucified. Paul, being a Roman citizen, was spared flogging and crucifixion; instead he was beheaded.

There was ample reason for Rome's reputation as a sink of corruption and iniquity as well as the imperial ruler of the world. Although Paul, in his letter to the Romans, was giving a description of the "world" in general that refused to recognize God and his law in created nature, it is clear that he also had Rome in mind as well as Corinth and other cities of the Empire when he wrote:

> The wrath of God is being revealed from heaven against the irreligious and perverse spirit of men who, in this perversity of theirs, hinder the truth. In fact whatever can be known about God is clear to them; he himself made it so. Since the creation of the world, invisible realities, God's eternal power and divinity, have become visible, recognized through the things he has made. Therefore, these men are inexcusable. They certainly had knowledge of God, yet they did not glorify him as God or give him thanks; they stultified themselves through speculating to no purpose, and their senseless hearts were darkened. They claimed to be wise but turned into fools instead; they exchanged the glory of the immortal God for images representing mortal men, birds, beasts and snakes. In consequence God gave them up in their lusts to unclean practices; they engaged in the

> mutual degradation of their bodies, these men who exchanged the truth of God for a lie. . . .
>
> Their women exchanged natural intercourse for unnatural, and the men gave up natural intercourse with women and burned with lust for one another. Men did shameful things with men and thus received in their own persons the penalty of their own perversity. They did not see fit to acknowledge God, so God delivered them up to their own depraved sense to do what is unseemly. They are filled with every kind of wickedness, maliciousness, great ill-will, envy, murder, bickering, deceit, craftiness. They are gossips and slanderers, they hate God, are insolent, haughty, boastful, ingenious in their wrongdoing, and rebellious toward their parents. One sees in them men without conscience, without loyalty, without affection, without pity. They know God's just decree that all who do such things deserve death.

Paul wrote his letter before he had come to Rome. There is general agreement that he wrote it from Corinth, in the hope that he would be able to visit Rome after he had delivered the collection of money to the Christians in Jerusalem. He did not anticipate that he would finally arrive at Rome as a prisoner. The violence that he feared and which he mentioned in his letter—"Pray that I may escape the unbelievers in Judea" (15:31—was actually unleashed on him and led to his appeal to the Roman authorities for protection. There is nothing in the letter that would reflect Paul's personal experience in Rome; he had not been there yet.

Actually Paul's letter to the Romans is not a pastoral

letter although it includes strong exhortations to the Christian life and ideals. It is a remarkable theological statement about God's plan of salvation, first to the Jews, then to the Gentiles. It represents the most careful and systematic presentation of God's relationship to his people. It has been a statement that has been at the heart of theological developments and controversies about salvation during the history of Christianity.

However, in Corinth Paul met some of the Jewish Christians who had been expelled from Rome in the time of Claudius, particularly Aquila and Priscilla, who were to become close collaborators in Paul's mission in Corinth and elsewhere. Aquila and Priscilla were tentmakers which indicates that some of the Jews in Rome were artisans like Paul himself. No doubt Paul heard much about the Christians in Rome from Priscilla and Aquila and others from Rome in Corinth who had been active in the Christian community in Rome. And it is clear that the Christians in Rome knew of Paul. They came out to greet him when he arrived as a prisoner in Rome and were apparently enthusiastic about his being present among them, even as a prisoner.

It was during his two years under house arrest that Paul came to know more about Rome and became acquainted with the Jewish community as well as the Christians, both Jews and Gentiles. His evangelizing efforts continued despite his confinement.

There was a large colony of Jews in Rome, estimated at about twenty thousand. They were a poor colony and lived in a section of the city called Subura, often referred to with disdain by Roman writers. Many of the Jews may have come to Rome after Pompey had conquered Jerusalem and brought them as captives to Rome. Occasionally they had problems with the emperors. They were exiled by Tiberius during the lifetime of Christ. They were exiled later by Claudius, apparently because of disturbances over Crestus, probably conflicts with Jews who had become Christians. Thus, unlike other cities where Jews were substantial middle class business people, in Rome they seem to have been a large but poor community. Some of them were Christians; Paul addressed his letter to them at Rome and he indicated that some of them met for prayers and the eucharist at the home of Aquila and Priscilla (Rom 16:3–5). But many were not Christians.

In his letter he mentions many of the Christians by name. It is not clear who each of them was. Epaenetus came from Asia, "the first of Asia's gifts to Christ." He speaks of Junius and Andronicus, "my compatriots and fellow prisoners who became Christians before me." He refers to another compatriot, Herodian, and to Rufus, who may have been the son of Simon of Cyrene. It is evident that some members of the community in Rome had come from distant places, either as slaves or freedmen or evangelists. The many other names in chapter 16 indicate a wide acquaintance of Paul with the Christians in Rome. They must have been a dedicated group. Paul tells them: "Your faith is spoken of all over the world" (1:8), and later: "Your faith in Christ, anyway, is famous everywhere" (16:19). He mentions in his letter that he ". . . hopes to find encouragement from them" (1:12).

There was evidently trouble between the Christian Jews and non-Christians. It is not clear what the complaints of Claudius were when he exiled the Jews. But there may have been problems among the Christians themselves. Paul says to them: "This is why you should never pass judgment on a brother or treat him with contempt, as some of you have done" (Rom 14:10), and later:

"Far from passing judgment on each other, therefore, you should make up your mind never to be the cause of your bother tripping or falling" (Rom 14:13). Some of the problems may have been about food, probably the food that may have been offered to the idols. Later in chapter 14, Paul makes that an issue once again, as he did in chapter 10 of his first letter to the Corinthians. His strong exhortation to Christian love and charity reflects his effort to support the unity and harmony of the Jewish Christians in Rome.

It is remarkable to note Paul's understanding and compassion, especially for those who were weak, and his concern for the freedom of individuals to serve the Lord according to their own conscience.

> People range from those who believe they may eat any sort of meat to those whose faith is so weak they dare not eat anything except vegetables. Meat eaters must not despise the scrupulous. On the other hand the scrupulous must not condemn those who feel free to eat anything they choose since God has welcomed them. . . . If one man keeps certain days as holier than others, and another considers all days to be equally holy, each must be left free to hold his own opinion. The one who observes special days does so in honor of the Lord. The one who eats meat does so in honor of the Lord, since he gives thanks to God (14:2–6).

Paul saw the different preferences of the Christians. He was most concerned that they not appropriate their own preference as obligatory on others. "If we live we live for the Lord; if we die we die for the Lord, so that, alive or dead, we belong to the Lord" (14:7–8). And his admonition: "So let us adopt any custom that leads to peace and mutual improvement; do not wreck God's work over a question of food" (14:19). "It can only be to God's glory, then, for you to treat each other in the same friendly way as Christ treated you" (15:7). There was his continuing emphasis on their unity in Jesus.

Yet there was the other question, how Paul came to a decision about what was permissible and what was not. The problem of food rose from two sources, a carry-over from the Hebrew dietary restrictions, and the practice of pagan Romans of offering food to their gods. Paul insisted that Christians who wished to take advantage of their freedom from the Mosaic law should be free to eat as they wished. Furthermore, from a practical point of view, Christians in a pagan world need not be concerned about what a host would place before them, whether it had been offered to idols or not. Paul saw these as minor issues which should not create division or controversy among Christians whose one guiding norm should be their union in Christ.

The first thing Paul did when he reached Rome was to invite the non-Christian Jews to meet with him and dialogue with him. Paul did not succeed in converting many and, as he did so often elsewhere, he cut himself off from them and spent his energies with the Gentiles.

The City of Rome

Rome was the capital city of the Roman empire, the most powerful city of the world at that time. Therefore, all the features of political power, economic influence, and social prestige were found here in the levels of government beginning with the emperor and descending through all the levels of an imperial bureaucracy. It was riddled with political intrigue, corruption and cruelty. The behavior of Nero, noted above, was only one aspect of the striving for power, privilege and wealth. There was the military, on which the security of the empire rested. The real power behind the throne of Nero was Tigellinus, the commander of Rome's military forces. Paul was guarded by a Roman soldier to whom he was chained. In this situation he was well aware of the Roman army and may have had converts among them during his house arrest.

There was the world of commerce, of wealth and economic power and influence. Rome had its own military-industrial complex, the network of industries and commercial arrangements that supported the Roman armies in the field and the vast bureaucracy that managed the control of the empire over its people. There were the slaves, many of whom were Greeks who served as teachers, cultural leaders, artists and musicians; there were the poor, some of them slaves, many of them freedmen, former slaves or foreigners who had migrated to Rome from the provinces, disenfranchised, poor, often exploited in their occupations, or unemployed and living on the dole. There were immigrants from all parts of the empire who crowded into the city, hoping to escape poverty, attracted by the fascination of a great city, or seeking some economic or social betterment. It was a mixture of nationalities, languages and cultures not unlike the lower east side of New York at the height of European immigration, or today with Italians, Hispanics, Chinese, Koreans and others. Paul found himself in the midst of this massive population of Rome. As Acts reports (28:30–32), in his own rented lodgings Paul welcomed all who came to visit him, proclaiming the kingdom of God and teaching the truth about the Lord Jesus

Christ with complete freedom and without hindrance from anyone.

The area in which Paul lived, probably the Subura, was what we would call today an inner city slum. It was marked by narrow streets, open sewers (a common feature of all ancient cities), poor housing, crowded conditions, but also by the intense human interaction and vitality of inner city slum areas. It was an area that wealthier and more sophisticated people avoided, and, knowing little about it, they probably had their myths about it as a dangerous and dismal section. Historians believe that Nero had the city burned in order to clear out this poor section. He had visions of rebuilding a magnificent urban area in its place. The fire got out of hand and, before it was controlled, it had destroyed a large part of the city of Rome, including many properties of the wealthy and prominent. At the same time, we know that it was inhabited by the early Christians who faced the heroic task of leading a Christian life in the presence of the dissolute society of Rome. It was to these people that Paul ministered, together with the Gentiles with whom he came into contact and who responded to the preaching of the gospel and became Christians.

Paul had written his letter to these Christians before he had come to Rome. As indicated above, his letter reflects what he knew of the Christian community at Rome; he may have had the Romans in mind when he wrote the severely critical description of fallen human nature in chapter 1 of his letter. At the same time, he commented on the exemplary lives of the Christians: "Your faith is spoken of all over the world," (1:8). Paul expects to bring them a gift of a deeper faith while, at the same time, he looks forward to finding among them an encouragement to himself to lead a life of deeper faith.

Paul's Relation to the People of Rome

What was the condition of the people to whom Paul ministered? Most of them were probably not Roman citizens as Paul was. Rome was an empire and all the people in the territories Rome had conquered were a subject, oppressed and exploited people. The evidence of this is abundant from the gospels. The Jews hated the Roman army of occupation and the tax collectors, the publicans, who with few exceptions, it appears, exploited the people in the process of collecting the taxes for Rome. What misled many of the Jews was their expectation that the messiah would deliver them from the oppression of the Romans who had conquered them. Much of the corruption of Jerusalem among the priests was related to the deals they made with Roman authorities to share in the lucrative business enterprises controlled by the Romans. This existed not only in Palestine but throughout the empire. Thus the poor people of Rome, whether slaves, or captives of war, or persons who had migrated to Rome hoping for a better living, were all subjects of the empire.

They had no vote. Rome was not a democracy. Nevertheless there was the remarkable institution of Roman law. The empire did not deal with its subject people arbitrarily. The law was clear and generally followed. Rome did have a system of due process. Note the swiftness of Roman intervention to protect Paul when he was attacked in Jerusalem, and the response of the Romans to his demand for due process. "You have appealed to Caesar; to Caesar you shall go" (Acts 25:12). However, many of the people in Rome were not citizens. The Jews, for example, were evicted from Rome more than once. They had been evicted by Tiberius, the emperor during the lifetime of Christ. Aquila and Priscilla, who met Paul in Corinth, had been among the Jews evicted by Claudius in the late 50s. Roman law was not very helpful in the presence of a man like Nero. He killed citizens and non-citizens alike in his madness.

Paul's Attitude Toward Civil Authorities

It is important to note Paul's attitude toward civil authorities. It is in this area that noticeable differences appear between Paul's instructions to the poor and exploited of his day in contrast to our approach to the poor in the inner cities of our day. Paul has the following strong and clear statement about political authorities in language quite different from what we would use today.

> You must all obey the governing authorities. Since all government comes from God, the civil authorities were appointed by God, and so anyone who resists authority is rebelling against God's decision, and such an act is bound to be punished. Good behavior is not afraid of magistrates; only criminals have anything to fear. If you want to live without being afraid of authority you must live honestly, and authority may even honor you. The state is there to serve God for your benefit. If you break the law, however, you may well have fear: the bearing of the sword has its significance. The authorities are there to serve God; they carry out God's revenge by punishing wrongdoers. You must obey, therefore, not only because you are afraid of being punished, but also for conscience's sake. This is also the reason why you must pay taxes, since all government officials are God's officers. They serve God by collecting taxes. Pay

every government official what he has a right to ask—whether it be direct tax or indirect, fear or honor.

Paul is evidently thinking in ideal terms about governing authorities. The early Christians conceived of authority as coming from God, conferred on rulers in quite a different process than the representative government which dominates our thinking today. In the Hebrew tradition, the king was consecrated much like the priest; the conferring of authority on him in the name of God had characteristics of a sacred rite. Kings were seen to have enormous responsibilities for governing the people with justice and righteousness. Psalm 72 depicts the ideal king who promotes the cause of justice and peace and who defends the poor:

God, give your own justice to the king,
your own righteousness to the royal son,
so that he may rule your people rightly
and your poor with justice.

Let the mountains and the hills
bring a message of peace to the people.
Uprightly he will defend the poorest,
he will save the children and those in need
and crush their oppressors.

Jesus emphasized respect for authority: "The scribes and Pharisees occupy the chair of Moses. You must do what they tell you and listen to what they say; but do not be guided by what they do, since they do not practice what they preach" (Mt 23:3–4). But Jesus is fierce in his condemnation of the injustice of the leaders of his time who inflicted heavy burdens on the people over whom they exercised authority.

> Alas for you scribes and Pharisees, you hypocrites! You who shut up the kingdom of heaven in men's faces, neither going in yourselves nor allowing others to go in who want to. Alas for you, scribes and Pharisees, you hypocrites! You who travel over sea and land to make a single proselyte, and when you have him you make him twice as fit for hell as you are.

Paul never launches out against religious or political leaders as Jesus did. It is not clear what instruction he would give if there were clear violations of civil rights as modern men and women would understand them. Paul must have been aware of the injustice and exploitation by the tax collectors in Palestine, the hated publicans. All he mentions is: "Pay every government official what he has a right to ask." When they asked more and pocketed it, what would Paul have said? And he was certainly aware of the corruption in Rome and elsewhere.

Furthermore, Paul and the early Christians expected a quick return of Jesus. Thus they were more concerned about preparing themselves for his coming than seeking to reform civil societies. Thus Paul's exhortation to the Christians was to keep themselves clear of the sinfulness of the world around them and lead lives of the followers of Jesus: "Do not model yourselves on the behavior of the world around you, but let your behavior change, modeled by our new mind. This is the only way to discover the will of God and know what is good, what it is that God wants, what is the perfect thing to do" (12:2).

> Besides, you must know "the time" has come: you must wake up now; our salvation is even nearer than it was when we were converted. The night is almost over, it will be daylight soon—let us give up all the things we prefer to do under cover of the dark; let us arm ourselves and appear in the light. Let us live decently as people do in the daytime: no drunken orgies, no promiscuity or licentiousness, and no wrangling or jealousy. Let your armor be the Lord Jesus Christ; forget about satisfying your bodies with all their cravings (13:11–14).

In this regard, Paul's perspective on justice was quite different from the approach of committed Catholics today. We do have drunkenness, and our public media saturate the environment with sex; wrangling and jealousy are widespread in poor communities as well as among the affluent. Add to this the horrible plague of drugs and the violence in the streets; there is plenty in our day similar to the problems of Paul's day, and some things worse, to which his condemnations would be appropriate.

However, the political, economic and social situations of our time are very different. We have representative government today, and we conceive of the authority that comes from God as conferred on public authorities by the vote of the people. If these authorities do not govern justly, or even effectively, the vote of the population can remove them and replace them. This type of responsiveness to the electorate was not prevalent in the time of Paul. In view of this, we are preoccupied with the way societies function and our responsibility to change them. Poverty, homelessness, exploitation in the workplace, denial of opportunity, prejudice and discrimination are the context in which we see the need for Christian responsibility. Thus concern for human rights and civil rights are seen as an essential part of ministry to the poor.

Paul sounds very different from the documents of the meeting of the Latin American bishops at Medellín in 1968 and Puebla in 1979: "We are at the beginning of a new historic epoch in our continent." The bishops concluded: "It is filled with hope of total emancipation—liberation from all servitude—personal maturity and collective integration. We see the painful gestation of a new civilization."[1]

"A deafening cry pours out from the throats of millions of people asking their pastors for a liberation that reaches them from nowhere else. Now you are listening to us in silence, but we hear the shout arising from your suffering," Pope Paul VI told the campesinos of Colombia.[2] This cry echoed throughout the world. Injustice and violence were seen as built into the structure of societies in Latin America and elsewhere. It was the insistence of the pope and of the bishops at Medellín that this had to be corrected. The Documents of the Thirty-Second Congregation of the Society of Jesus repeats this challenge: "It is by this we know that the promotion of justice is an integral part of the priestly service of the faith."[3] Equally significant is the extraordinary statement of the Second Synod of Bishops in 1971: "Action on behalf of justice and participation in the transformation of the world fully appear to us as a constitutive dimension of the preaching of the gospel, or, in other words, of the church's mission for the redemption of the human race and its liberation from every oppressive situation."[4]

The recent letter of the American bishops about the American economy certainly repeats many things Paul says about the need to live a moral life: "The commandments to love God with all one's heart and to love one's neighbor as oneself are the heart and soul of Christian morality" (#64). But the letter speaks later (#73):

> Economic conditions that leave large numbers of people unemployed, underemployed, or employed in dehumanizing conditions fail to meet the converging demands of the three forms of basic justice. Work with adequate pay for all who seek it is the primary means for achieving basic justice in our society. Discrimination in job opportunities or income levels on the basis of race, sex, or other arbitrary standards can never be justified. It is a scandal that such discrimination continues in the United States today.

Obviously the bishops as well as the pope in his recent encyclical perceive Christian responsibility on quite a different perspective from that of Paul. In this regard Paul does not provide much help for the chronic social dislocations of our day. Political and social action are seen as important Christian responsibilities in a way in which Paul never spoke of them.

What Paul does teach us, and it can be effective in our day, is the fulfillment of the commandment of love in the presence of a world that in many ways is hostile to Jesus and the gospel. The first chapter of Romans cited above reflects Paul's criticism of the evils of the world of his time. Some of his severe criticisms could be stated about the world of our times:[5] "If you love your fellow men you have carried out your obligations. . . . Love is the one thing that cannot hurt your neighbor; that is why it is the answer to every one of the commandments" (Rom 13:8–10). He certainly speaks in the spirit of the words of Jesus, "Bless those who persecute you; never curse them; bless them. . . . Never repay evil with evil but let everyone see that you are interested only in the highest ideals. . . . If your enemy is hungry you should give him food, and if he be thirsty let him drink. . . . Resist evil and conquer it with good" (Rom 12:14-21).

> Glory to him who is able to give you the strength to live according to the good news I preach, and in which I proclaim Jesus Christ, the revelation of a mystery kept secret for endless ages, but now so clear that it must be broadcast to pagans everywhere to bring them to the obedience of faith. This is only what scripture has predicted, and it is all part of the way the eternal God wants things to be. "He alone is wisdom; give glory therefore to him through Jesus Christ for ever and ever. Amen."

Thus Paul was not concerned about many of the inner city issues which preoccupy us today, homes for the homeless, jobs for the unemployed, improvement of education, safety on the streets, the correction of the drug problem. His primary concern was the community of Christians in Christ Jesus. In this regard he would have much to say to inner city populations; community—especially community in Christ—is the critical need.

It is the sacred mystery hidden in God that will bring to the Christians of Rome and the inner city people of our day the grace they need: "Both Jew and pagan sinned and forfeited God's glory, and both are justified through the free gift of his grace by being redeemed in Christ Jesus who was appointed by God to sacrifice his life so as to win reconciliation through faith (3:24-25). Gentile as well as Jew, slave as well as free, women as well as men, were to be one in Jesus Christ. This Paul would preach to the people of our day: neither American nor Asian, nor Hispanic nor Indian, nor Korean nor Filipino, but only Christ Jesus. If this awareness of their unity in Jesus could be grasped and lived, prejudice and bias would disappear from the inner city; love would replace hostility, and the Christian community would emerge in which the problems that beset us would slowly give way to the love that each would have for the other in Christ. This sounds naive to the cynics of today. But Paul did it. And if we have the faith for which Paul prayed, he is convinced that it is as possible in our day as it was in his.

Notes

1. Latin American Episcopal Conference (CELAM), *The Church in the Present Day Transformation of Latin America in the Light of the Council* (Aptdo Aereo 5278, Bogota, D.E. Colombia, South America, 1970), Vol. 1, p. 9.

2. Address of Paul VI to the peasants at Mosquera, Colombia, August 23, 1968, Quoted in Latin American Episcopal Conference, *ibid.*, Vol. 2, p. 213.

3. Documents of the Thirty-Second General Congregation of the Society of Jesus, 12/2/74–3/7/75. Saint Louis: Institute of Jesuit Sources, 1977, part 4, #18.

4. "Justice in the World," Synod of Bishops, Second General Assembly, November 30, 1971, in Joseph Gremillion, ed., *The Gospel of Peace and Justice.* Maryknoll: Orbis, 1976, p. 514. This has been modified in subsequent statements, but the commitment to justice remains a clearly stated part of the church's mission.

5. It must be remembered that Paul spoke in the idiom of his own day. For example, were he speaking today of homosexuality, his language would probably reflect the perception of that behavior which is more common today.

7. The Apostolate in the Inner City

The challenge of today is not Antioch, Corinth or Rome. It is the inner city populations of New York, Chicago, Detroit, Philadelphia and others. These are the populations of the modern poor. They are predominantly black, Puerto Rican, and Asians, with a remnant of earlier immigrants from Europe and the near east. They are not the conquered peoples of an imperial power; they are immigrants like many of the residents of Rome, Corinth, Antioch and other cities of the empire. They are not slaves, although black Americans came from a history of slavery more brutal and dehumanizing than the slavery of Rome. Many of them, like many of the people of Paul's time, are not citizens, but they do enjoy a measure of civil rights; many are so called "illegal" residents who live in the shadows in the fear of being detected and deported. Most of them are poor, some of them very poor.

Many of them are baptized Catholics who have little knowledge of the faith; others are Christian, members of a variety of Protestant churches from Baptist to Pentecostal; others are from religions strange to the west: Hindus from India, Buddhists from Asia, devotees of Santeria from Cuba. They have an elemental sense of religion, that sense among the poor that the world has a meaning, that a supernatural power exists, that one we call God does care for us.

Problems Different or Similar?

This book was designed to call attention to Paul's response to the inner city population of his day with the hope that this would give us some helpful insights to guide us in our response to the inner city populations of our time. Briefly, what are the differences and similarities and what can Paul teach us about approaching the modern poor?

1. *The great difference: the service of the faith by the promotion of justice;* "the preferential option for the poor."
2. Perspectives on "community"; the "covenanted people" of Paul in the perspective of modern concepts of "community."
3. Life in Christ: the sacredness of the person.
4. Some pastoral reflections.

The problems of the modern poor are familiar. There is the scandal of homelessness; New York alone has an estimated 35,000 people with no place to live and no one to care for them. They suffer the problems of poor health: overcrowded hospitals, endless day-long waits in emergency rooms, casual discharges without care. They become victims of the modern plague: drug abuse and addiction, with the fatal consequence, in many cases, of AIDS. Those who are employed are in menial, poor-paying jobs which leave them below the officially defined poverty level. Their children do poorly in school, half of them dropping out before they finish, to face a life of unemployment or employment in similar menial occupations. They live in an environment of crime and violence. Many of their daughters become pregnant as teenagers. The litany of problems can go on and on. Yet, among these people there is often an impressive generosity, an ability to endure hardship, to survive. They are the modern poor, the by-product of the competitiveness of a capitalist society. They are the inhabitants of our modern "inner cities."

There are welfare programs, public housing for some, job-training programs, Medicaid for the poor and Medicare for the elderly—a wide range of public services. But with the enormous and expensive public effort to find a remedy, the problems seem to get worse. New York in 1988 broke all previous records for homicides, almost half of them related to drug trafficking. Most of all, they are increasingly segregated from the more affluent middle class. New York City, for example, between 1970 and 1980 lost 1,750,000 residents of white, European background. They moved to the all-white suburbs where citizens will effectively protest any effort to bring the poor, the handicapped, the homeless to decent shelters. As a result, less than twenty percent of the children in the entire public school system of New York City are white; seventy-three percent are black and Hispanic, seven percent Asian or other. In some cities like Hartford, Connecticut, the public school population is over ninety-five percent Hispanic and black. Creating communities of whites, blacks and Hispanics is difficult in the face of this new segregation.

This is a very different world in many ways from the inner cities of Saint Paul's time, yet there are similarities, a yearning for someone to respect them, to see in them persons worthy of some honor and attention, not in the bureaucratic services of public agencies, but in the form of personal attention by people who seek to know them and eventually love them. This is where the example of Paul can be so helpful. In some ways, Antioch, Corinth and Rome had more problems than modern inner cities. But Paul, as we have seen, was able to find in them the sources of rich spiritual and religious development. What help can we get from Paul?

The Poverty of Corinth vs. Poverty in the South Bronx

Paul never spoke of the poor of his day in economic or political terms. We never cease speaking about it in those terms. The poor of our day, residents of the south Bronx, for example, are people who have little money and suffer the consequences of not having it; they are also the people who have limited power over institutions, public or private, on which their lives depend. This has been defined by American bishops as a situation that is unjust, and our commitment to the faith involves a commitment to bring about justice for the poor. The bishops of South America at Medellín in 1968 declared a "preferential option for the poor" in order to fulfill the call to the imitation of Jesus:

> The spirit of the Lord has been given to me,
> for he has anointed me.
> He has sent me to bring the good news to the
> poor,
> to proclaim liberty to captives
> and to the blind new sight,
> to set the downtrodden free,
> to proclaim the Lord's year of favor (Lk 4:18).

The great revolution of the church especially in South and Central America has been its deep involvement in the drive for social and political changes which will remedy the intolerable condition of the poor and bring about a more just society. The official statements of the church for the past century, in the encyclicals and the documents of Vatican II, are a consistent and emphatic call for a just political and social order.

The evangelization of the poor, therefore, is seen in much broader terms than Paul ever envisioned it: political and social action for change, housing programs, educational efforts, job-training and assistance in getting employment, programs for health improvement, for betterment of the criminal justice system, for assistance to immigrants and refugees, and many other services. One thinks in contrast of Paul's constant but individual efforts to collect money for the needy Christians in Jerusalem. Paul's preaching sometimes led to upheavals such as the protests of the silver merchants in Ephesus, and the occasional riots of the Jews who opposed his preaching about Jesus. But these were provoked by his doctrine. He was never involved in what we would recognize as social and political action to bring about justice for the poor.

This change in perspective is due largely to the different historical situations. As indicated above, Paul lived at a time when Christians, including himself, anticipated an early return of Jesus to the earth. As a result, they were mainly preoccupied about being prepared for his coming by an intense spiritual life, and by a rejection of the "world" in the sense in which Jesus had used it, namely, that spirit which rejected his Gospel and denied his identity as the messiah, the Son of God. History has changed this perspective. We are much more aware today of the meaning of the words of Jesus, "But as for that day or hour, nobody knows it, neither the angels of heaven, nor the Son, no one but the Father" (Mk 13:32). The mystery of salvation has unfolded during two thousand years and leaves us more uncertain than ever about the ways God's providence will manifest itself in the future. Furthermore the emergence of the knowledge of the human family has revealed to us the wonders of God's creation that were not dreamed of in the time of Paul. The Constitution on the Church in the Modern World of Vatican II is a proclamation of the wonders of God's creation and the challenge to the church to fulfill itself in relation to that aspect of the world as seen as the manifestation of God's glory in contrast to the spirit of evil which is at work in the world to reject Jesus.

Secondly, the history of the church has revealed the conflict between good and evil—evil that has often invaded the intimate life of the church itself—and the church is very conscious today of its own involvement in evil at certain moments of its history. It recognizes in the bitter suffering of so many of God's children the consequences of evil and injustice which prevent men and women from fulfilling in their lives the image of himself that God created in them. Thus, the "preferential option for the poor" is seen as a feature of the mission of Jesus to the world. If modern evangelists are to imitate Jesus, they are aware of the preference they must show for the poor. Furthermore the abundance of our knowledge today of the causes of poverty, injustice and oppression leaves us with an awareness of our responsibility in the spirit of the gospel to correct the injustices which exist. The fulfillment of the gospel involves the pursuit of justice.

There is no way of telling what Paul would do if he came to the south Bronx instead of Corinth. There is no doubt that he would recognize in the people there the potential for spiritual and religious enrichment; he would stir in them a profound sense of their importance as members of the body of Christ. He would be convinced that if his followers lived a life in Jesus and with

Jesus as a community of Christians, change would inevitably follow. He would recognize, as we do today, that the second coming of Jesus may be ages away, but conversion to a life with Jesus would eventually do away with divisions between blacks and whites, Hispanics and Asians; they would all be one in Christ Jesus.

It is very likely that he would meet the same kinds of divisions and jealousies, conflicts and resistance such as he met in Antioch, Corinth, and Jerusalem. But if we can judge from his activity in the Roman cities, he would be incredibly patient, enduring the personal animosity and abuse, showing love and forgiveness, seeking to bring all to an awareness of their oneness in Christ.

Community

If all lived in Christ and Christ lived in them, the community of Christians was formed, and Paul never ceased to emphasize the central importance of community in Christ. "You must live your whole life according to the Christ you have received—Jesus the Lord; you must be rooted in him and built on him and held firm by the faith you have been taught, and full of thanksgiving" (Col 2:6). Paul compared the community of Christians to a body: "Just as a human body, though it is made up of many parts, is a single unit because all these parts, though many, make one body, so it is with Christ. In the one Spirit we are all baptized, Jews as well as Greeks, slaves as well as citizens, and one Spirit was given to us all to drink" (1 Cor 12:12-13). Some of the most beautiful statements of Paul are his exhortations to show love for one another in a community of Christians.

> You are God's chosen ones, his saints; he loves you, and you should be clothed in sincere compassion, in kindness and humility, gentleness

> and patience. Bear with one another; forgive each other as soon as a quarrel begins. The Lord has forgiven you; now you must do the same. Over all these clothes, to keep them together and complete them, put on love. And may the peace of Christ reign in your hearts, because it is for this that you were called together as parts of one body. Always be thankful (Col 3:12-15).

No matter how crude or sinful his disciples had been, and his descriptions of them indicate that they were difficult people to deal with, his confidence in them, but more so his confidence in the grace of Christ, enabled him to preach a gospel of Christian community. Christ had prayed: "That all may be one, Father, as you and I are one," and Paul taught that day-in and day-out to his followers.

We may become discouraged today in our efforts to help the poor to realize the greatness of their being, or to live in peace and harmony with one another—the term "burn-out" has become a common expression among those who work with the poor—but the experience of Paul gives us the assurance that, if taught emphatically and enthusiastically, the poor respond.

> Bear with one another charitably, in complete selflessness, gentleness and patience. Do all you can to preserve the unity of the Spirit by the peace that binds you together. There is one body, one Spirit, just as you were all called into one and the same hope when you were called. There is one Lord, one faith, one baptism, and one God who is the Father of all, over all, through all and within all (Eph 4:2-6).

Despite the beautiful exhortations, it was not easy for Paul to keep the community together. Divisions were always breaking out. The letters to the Corinthians are a litany of problems he had to deal with; he found himself in opposition even to Peter at Antioch; he warns the Galatians not to allow enmities to tear the community apart. We should not feel any more discouraged than he if we face the problem of maintaining unity in the inner city communities of our day.

Theologically, we are a "covenanted" people, a people that God calls his own, a family—the Hebrews first during the period of preparation, Christians thereafter in the community of those who are one in Christ. As the Second Vatican Council expresses it:

> "Behold the days shall come, saith the Lord, and I will make a new covenant with the house of Israel, and with the house of Judah. . . . I will give my law in their bowels and I will write it in their heart; and I will be their God and they shall be my people. . . . For all shall know me, from the least of them even to the greatest, saith the Lord" (Jer 31:31-34). Christ instituted this new covenant, that is to say, the new testament, in His blood (cf. 1 Cor 11:25) by calling together a people made up of Jew and Gentile, making them one, not according to the flesh but in the Spirit.
>
> This was to be the new people of God. For those who believe in Christ, who are reborn not from a perishable but from an imperishable seed through the word of the living God (cf. 1 Pet 1:23) not from the flesh but from water and the Holy Spirit (cf. Jn 3:5-6), are finally estab-

> lished as "a chosen race, a royal priesthood, a holy nation, a purchased people . . . you who in times past were not a people, but are now a people of God" (1 Pet 2:9-10). (*Dogmatic Constitution on the Church (Lumen Gentium)* Ch. II, #9, in Walter M. Abbott, S.J., ed., *The Documents of Vatican II*, New York: Herder, 1966, p. 25).

Thus, in the official wording of the church, the reality of the community of Christians is clearly defined as a "people," united with God in a sacred covenant, struck in the blood of Jesus Christ. What is significant in the life of Paul is to see the way he brought this about amongst a population that most intelligent people would have called hopeless and unpromising. The history and letters of Paul describe in detail the resistance, the conflicts and jealousies, the hostility that Paul had to overcome in order to bring about the community of Christians. To the very end he was still struggling with them, discouraged because at the very end, as he says, "Every one of them deserted me" (2 Tim 4:16). The important thing is the encouragement that Paul gives us, his complete commitment to the task of creating the community of Christians, and our confidence that, following his example, we may have similar success.

Community today is not only an ecclesiastical concept and term. It is a basic concept in all sociological literature, a recognition by social scientists of the basic necessity of community in human societies. It is true that the sociological concept of community would embrace the church, a covenanted people, and sociologists would acknowledge that, as a community, the church fulfills for its members the socio-psychological satisfactions of community without which no social group can have stability. The community provides a sense of common identity, a spontaneous awareness of common values, a deep sense of dependence on one another for the fulfillment of human needs, a shared sense of common goals and common symbols that express the meaning that life has for the members of the social group. The symbol of cleansing and communication of life in the waters of baptism; the central symbols of the bread and wine at the celebration of the eucharist and the unity of the faithful in the body and blood of Jesus; the symbols of oil and the laying on of hands; the unity of husband and wife as a symbol of the union of Christ with his church—all these powerful symbols convey the satisfaction of community that enrich the lives of the "people of God." What sociologists at a much later time discovered as an essential feature of a stable community, Paul had preached and achieved among the poor in the inner cities of the Roman empire.

Therefore today we have not only the example of Paul and the official definitions of the church; we also have the insights of modern social scientists that the satisfactions of community are essential for a complete human life. The fullness of community is achieved in the unity of Christians in Christ. Paul had the vision long before modern social science discovered it.

Basic Christian Communities

The most determined effort to achieve Christian communities today are the *comunidades de base* as they are called, basic Christian communities. These flourish in South and Central America more than in the United States. They are found among Hispanics more so than among other ethnic groups. They are small groups of Catholics, generally from the same neighborhood, who gather to pray, to read the gospel and reflect on it. They are frequently composed of all lay people, guided by trained leaders called "delegates of the word." They have been a source of the renewal of vitality to Catholic life. The participants reflect on the meaning the gospel has for them in the circumstances of their lives, their obligation to bring the life and word of Jesus to their neighbors, their obligation to come to the assistance of neighbors who are in need.

Where situations of oppression and injustice exist, the members of the *comunidades*, as their brothers' and sisters' keepers, may feel obliged to become active in social and political action to bring about a change in unjust social structures. This has often resulted in violent opposition by people of power and privilege. Thousands have been murdered in Central and South America.

Paul himself was repeatedly attacked, indeed nearly killed on many occasions. He offered himself as an example to Christians who would face suffering, and he would certainly speak with encouragement to the Christians who die for the faith in today's turmoils:

> Nothing therefore can come between us and the love of Christ, even if we are troubled or worried, or being persecuted or lacking food or clothes, or being threatened or even attacked. As scripture promised: *For your sake we are being massacred daily, and reckoned as sheep for the slaughter.* These are the trials through which we triumph, by the power of him who loved us. For I am certain of this, that neither death nor life, no angel, no prince, nothing that exists, nothing that is to come, not any power,

> or height or depth, nor any created thing can come between us and the love of God made visible in Christ Jesus, our Lord (Rom 8:35-39).

The suffering of Christians for justice has not reached the point of dying in the United States. But Paul's words would be a support not only for those who suffer and die in Central and South America, but for all who struggle for justice and peace in the United States and suffer arrest or persecution or painful opposition. They are aware that the bond of faith unites them in Christ as members of a Christian community that seeks to serve the neighbor after the example of Christ.

The Value of Each Person in Christ

The first thing that impresses anyone who studies Saint Paul is his recognition of the greatness of each person in Christ Jesus. "You are, all of you, sons of God through faith in Christ Jesus. All baptized in Christ, you have all clothed yourselves in Christ, and there are no more distinctions between Jew and Greek, slave and free, male and female, but all of you are one in Christ Jesus" (Gal 3:26-28). Paul knew the value of every person, Jew and pagan, who was redeemed by Christ. He begged all to see this and to search in each person for the qualities which would enable them to respond to the call of God to salvation. "Finally, brothers, fill your minds with everything that is true, everything that is noble, everything that is good and pure, everything that we love and honor, and everything that can be thought virtuous or worthy of praise. . . . Then the God of peace will be with you" (Phil 4:8-9). "You have stripped off your old behavior with your old self, and you have put on a new self which will progress toward true knowledge the more it is renewed in the image of its creator; and in that image there is no room for distinction between Greek and Jew, between the circumcised and the uncircumcised, or between barbarian and Scythian, slave and free man. . . . There is only Christ; he is everything and he is in everything" (Col 3:11).

Paul would see in every person in the slums of the inner city someone capable of being redeemed by Christ, who could live in Christ and with Christ. Once the poor have a sense of that respect, the reverence that someone is showing them, their sense of importance can burst into life and give them a new way of being.

Paulo Freire, the great Brazilian educator, often told the story of a Brazilian peasant to whom he was teaching literacy. In one evening of instruction he was able to teach the man to write, and he wrote his own name. The man stood there in amazement, then turned to Freire and said: "I know now for the first time that I am a man, because I have written my own name." It seems that the poor of the Roman cities must have had similar experiences once they realized in response to Paul's preaching that they were important, that they bore within themselves the image of God, that they had been saved by Christ. We all know how enthusiastically we respond to someone who regards us as important. This was certainly the response of the poor to Paul's preaching. It would be the response of the inner city poor of today if they become aware that we recognize their importance.

If there is anything needed in the inner cities of today, it is the recognition of the poor as persons of worth and dignity. The modern institutions which have been created to serve them, to help them fulfill their lives, have become such depersonalized bureaucracies that they have created more problems for the poor than they have solved. One thinks often of Willowbrook, an institution for the chronically mentally handicapped in Staten Island, New York. It was declared a human warehouse by the courts who gave orders that its inmates were to be removed as soon as possible. The first children were removed to a project in the Bronx where they lived as a small group in a beautiful apartment under the care of house parents and staff who gave them attention they had never received. In a very short time, the children came to life, showed remarkable improvement and ability to function in society, and eventually were able to return to the homes of their parents. However, at the same time, psychological and psychiatric consultants recommended the deinstitutionalization of thousands of inmates of hospitals for the mentally handicapped. They were released on their own to neighborhoods around the city with no adequate community supports. They have become the abandoned, the exploited and the homeless of today. The poor face the day-long waiting in crowded emergency rooms. The thousands of children who drop out of school complain that they never felt that they meant anything to anyone. The list could be continued for pages.

The programs which have succeeded in giving the poor an awareness that their worth as persons was being recognized have discovered how quickly the hidden abilities of the poor begin to show themselves. The response to personal attention, respect and love can work miracles.

Thus the example of Paul and his preaching of the value of each person in Christ is essential today if the hidden potential of the poor is to be fulfilled. It was fulfilled in his day in remarkable and unexpected developments. This gives us hope that it could be fulfilled in the inner cities of today.

> Out of his infinite glory, may he give you the power through his Spirit for your *hidden self* to grow strong, so that Christ may live in your hearts through faith, and then, planted in love and built on love, you will with all the saints have strength to grasp the breadth and the length, the height and the depth until, knowing the love of Christ, which is beyond all knowledge, you are filled with the utter fullness of God. Glory to him whose power, working in us, can do infinitely more than we can ask or imagine (Eph 3:16-20). (Italics mine.)

There is a *hidden self* in each of us that can become fulfilled in the utter fullness of God. But the intermediary to enable the poor persons to realize this love that God has for them must be ourselves. If we can achieve that by communicating to the poor our recognition of the value of their inner self, we may find in the people of our inner cities a creativeness and a potential for spiritual and religious growth that will be surprising.

Some Pastoral Reflections

It is clear from previous chapters that Paul had to make many decisions about living a Christian life in a Jewish or a pagan world. His conviction about the freedom from the Mosaic law brought him into controversy not only with non-Christian Jews, but with many Christian Jews as well. That was a basic and most important decision. Paul's commitment to the freedom of the Gentiles was discussed earlier in Chapter 1. But there were many other issues that he faced and which required deciding about the way Christians should behave in a pagan world. Some of these are also mentioned above. What forms of expected behavior were acceptable to Christianity? It is in this regard that the pastoral style of Paul can be seen and his pastoral care of the people to whom he ministered. He and his disciples were the first ones to face this issue. They had no precedent to guide them apart from the religious experience of the Jewish people.

In this regard, Paul's decisions about the behavior of Christians were quite different from our experience today after centuries of Christian life. We are living today in a nation that calls itself Christian, and the great majority of people in the inner cities today are Christian. Decisions today are decisions about changes in the church (Vatican II, for example) or on modifications of Christian moral teachings in view of the new knowledge that is emerging (biomedical ethics, for example) and the cultural changes which are occurring not only in the United States but elsewhere in the world. Difficult as these decisions may be, we have the background of centuries of Christian experience and the guidance of a wide range of moral authorities. Thus, when we seek in the experience of Paul some light or insight about teaching the people of our modern "inner cities," we must be aware of the particular circumstances in which Paul was teaching and which prompted a style and manner that may not be suitable today.

In the first place, Paul had lived in a Jewish culture, and many of his attitudes and judgments such as the behavior of women at the Christian assemblies (1 Cor 11) were simply a continuation of Jewish religious traditions, or a reflection of Greek and Roman cultural practices such as the acceptance of slavery. His language which often strikes us as very harsh reflects a style of speaking found commonly in the psalms (smash the heads of their children on a rock) and the language Jesus used in his condemnation of the scribes and Pharisees (Mt 23).

There is no spirit of ecumenism found in Paul's teachings. He was convinced that he possessed the truth—God had revealed it to him, and no deviation from it was to be tolerated: ". . . and let me warn you that if anyone preaches a version of the good news different from the one we have already preached to you, whether it be ourselves or an angel from heaven, he is to be condemned" (Gal 1:8). "Make sure that no one traps you and deprives you of your freedom by some second-hand, empty, rational philosophy based on the principles of this world instead of on Christ" (Col 2:8). Paul had to be very firm in his rejection of the Jews, Christian or non-Christian, who wanted to impose the Mosaic law on the Gentiles. There was the revelation to Peter (Acts 10), the council of Jerusalem (Acts 15) and his own enlightenment from God (Gal 1:11-12). He was compelled to reject anyone who refused to respect the freedom of the Gentiles from the Mosaic law. His powerful statement in the letter to the Galatians, insisting that they reject anyone who seeks to impose the law on the Gentiles, indicates Paul's inflexible conviction that life in Jesus had replaced the law as the source of our salvation.

But the rejection of false teachers went beyond the issue of freedom from the law. Paul lived at a time when Christians were surrounded by all kinds of pagan rites or religious sects and dogmas. There was always the risk that Christians would be attracted to some kind of new teaching and be drawn from their faith in Christ. As the second letter to Timothy puts it: "The time is sure to come when, far from being content with sound teaching, people will be avid for the lastest novelty and collect themselves a whole series of teachers according to their own taste; and then, instead of listening to the truth, they will turn to myths" (2 Tim 4:3-4). Paul had to struggle hard to protect the early Christian churches. The thrill of the "good news" of Jesus was so inspiring ("I pray kneeling before the Father in amazement and wonder at the mystery of it all" (Eph 3:14), he could not see how people could be attracted to the cults around them. But it is understandable that he had to be excessively firm for the protection of the flock.

The circumstances of the modern inner cities are very different from those of Paul's time. Most of the people in our inner cities come from a Christian background. There are blacks from Baptist or Methodist backgrounds, or Hispanics from a Catholic background. There are numerous Pentecostal and Evangelical groups. The great challenge to all churches is evangelization, bringing a more active and informed religious experience to the poor. Catholics find it necessary to protect their own people from the aggressive proselytizing of Pentecostal sects. The basic form of protection is an effective evangelization of Catholics so that they will understand the difference between Catholicism and the other Christian sects and denominations, an effort which has never been adequate. Large numbers of baptized Catholics are attracted to the Pentecostal and Evangelical sects by the sense of community they find there in the smaller, more intimate congregations and the involvement in the scriptures which they do not always find in the Catholic Church.[1] The Pentecostals and Evangelicals resist any ecumenical relationship. Thus there is a need to create within Catholic parishes an experience of community, a religious style where the poor feel completely at home. Some of the Pentecostal churches are openly hostile to the Catholic Church, accusing it of being a false religion that has lost the Spirit of Christ and the gospels. As indicated above, the features of Catholicism as a "covenant people," as the "body of Christ," as a community, become essential in the response to the people of the inner city. In this regard, the remarkable teachings of Paul can be inspiring and helpful.

Relations to the denominational churches, Baptist, Methodist, etc., are different from that of the Pentecostals and Evangelicals. Here more of an ecumenical spirit prevails. There is the longing and the prayer for an eventual reunification of Christianity that results in more friendly discussion and celebration of the churches. They are constantly cooperating in community efforts to improve housing, care for the homeless, prevent drug traffic and drug use, protect the neighborhood, and improve the conditions of life. In these efforts, participants find themselves saying the same prayers, singing the same hymns, raising the same petitions to God. An awareness of common faith and unity in religious practice constitutes an ongoing ecumenical spirit that may make dialogue much easier. No similar situation existed in the time of Paul.

Moral Teaching

Paul's moral teaching was similar to that of the Jewish teaching of his time.

> When self-indulgence is at work the results are obvious: fornication, gross indecency and sex-

> ual irresponsibility; idolatry and sorcery; feuds and wrangling; jealousy, bad temper and quarrels; disagreements, factions, envy; drunkenness, orgies and similar things. I warn you now as I warned you before, those who behave like this will not inherit the kingdom of God. What the spirit brings is very different: love, joy, peace, patience, kindness, goodness, trustfulness, gentleness and self-control. There can be no law against that, of course. You cannot belong to Christ Jesus unless you crucify all self-indulgent passions and desires (Gal 5:19-24).

Paul repeats these moral proclamations frequently in various contexts. Of course, there is the severe condemnation of the immorality of "the world" in Romans 1. It is surprising to contrast Paul's moral statements against those of Jesus. Paul never refers to what we would call "social injustice" unless these are implied in the extract above. Jesus is very explicit: the Pharisees and scribes are condemned for placing heavy burdens on the shoulders of the poor (Mt 23:4); they have neglected the weightier matters of the law—justice, mercy, good faith (Mt 23:23). The parable of the unforgiving debtor dealt with debt and forgiveness of debt (Mt 18:23-35); there is the parable of the day laborers and their pay (Mt 20), and the parable of the rich man and Lazarus (Lk 16:19-31). The ones "blest of my Father" who are called to eternal life are those who fed the hungry, gave drink to the thirsty, gave a home to the homeless, etc. (Mt. 25:14-30). It is possible that since Paul was speaking to ordinary citizens living in a pagan and corrupt world, he emphasized principles of personal morality whereas Jesus was speaking to scribes and Pharisees who had authority over the people. But the sermon on the mount (Mt 5–6), the description of the last judgment and the parables were addressed to ordinary people.

The statements of Paul would certainly be in place today. The enormity of drug and alcohol addiction in the United States, the violence of the cities, the rate of homicides, teenage pregnancy and out-of-wedlock births, rape and child abuse are situations which prompt strong moral preaching, and the style of Paul's preaching would be appropriate.

However the strong moral preaching was always associated with guidance and counsel that reflect a great sensitivity to the moral problems facing inner city populations and a very human perspective in approaching them.

At the end of the second letter to Timothy, the sad words of Paul are reported: "The first time I had to present my defense, there was not a single witness to support me. Every one of them had deserted me—may they not be held accountable for it." Time after time, Paul had suffered disappointment and discouragement, betrayal and opposition. It is the final suggestion of his message that anyone working with the people of the inner city must also expect disappointment and discouragement, as the Lord Jesus had experienced it. In the garden of Gethsemani, the gospel tells us, "All the disciples deserted him and ran away" (Mt 26:56). Paul offers us no consolation that all is going to be bright, despite the wonderful successes of his apostolate. In the long run we must be prepared for discouragement. However that is not the last word: "But the Lord stood by me and gave me power, so that through me the whole message might be proclaimed for all the pagans to hear; and so I was *rescued from the lion's mouth.* The Lord will rescue me from all evil attempts on me, and bring me safely to his heavenly kingdom. To him be glory for ever and ever. Amen" (2 Tim 4:17-18). The apostolate to the inner city will not be easy: it will be marked by disappointment and discouragement. But Paul's final word was, "The Lord stood by me and gave me power." And to those in the inner cities of our day, the Lord will be the one great source of power.

Note

1. Allan Figueroa Deck, S. J., "Proselytism and Hispanic Catholics: How Long Can We Cry Wolf?" *America*, Dec. 10, 1988, pp. 485–490. See also, J. Juan Diaz Vilar, S.J., "The Success of the Sects Among Hispanics in the United States," *America*, Feb. 25, 1989, pp. 174–181.